CHRIST-CENTERED

Exposition

AUTHOR David Platt
SERIES EDITORS David Platt, Daniel L. Akin, and Tony Merida

CHRIST-CENTERED
Exposition

EXALTING JESUS IN

JAMES

HOLMAN®
REFERENCE
BRENTWOOD, TENNESSEE

SERIES DEDICATION

Dedicated to Adrian Rogers and John Piper. They have taught us to love the gospel of Jesus Christ, to preach the Bible as the inerrant Word of God, to pastor the church for which our Savior died, and to have a passion to see all nations gladly worship the Lamb.

—David Platt, Tony Merida, and Danny Akin
March 2013

TABLE OF CONTENTS

ACKNOWLEDGMENTS

This commentary is the fruit of God's grace in the lives of many brothers and sisters. I am especially grateful to God for Cory Varden, who consistently and graciously serves alongside me, and David Burnette, who has taken my sermon manuscripts and edited them for the chapters of this commentary. I am ever grateful to God for Heather as well as Caleb, Joshua, Mara Ruth, and Isaiah; I am blessed beyond measure with the family He has entrusted to me. And I am deeply grateful to God for The Church at Brook Hills, a faith family who eagerly opened their Bibles every week not only to hear but also to obey the voice of God in James for the glory of God among the nations.

David Platt

SERIES INTRODUCTION

Augustine said, "Where Scripture speaks, God speaks." The editors of the Christ-Centered Exposition Commentary series believe that where God speaks, the pastor must speak. God speaks through His written Word. We must speak from that Word. We believe the Bible is God breathed, authoritative, inerrant, sufficient, understandable, necessary, and timeless. We also affirm that the Bible is a Christ-centered book; that is, it contains a unified story of redemptive history of which Jesus is the hero. Because of this Christ-centered trajectory that runs from Genesis 1 through Revelation 22, we believe the Bible has a corresponding global-missions thrust. From beginning to end, we see God's mission as one of making worshipers of Christ from every tribe and tongue worked out through this redemptive drama in Scripture. To that end we must preach the Word.

In addition to these distinct convictions, the Christ-Centered Exposition Commentary series has some distinguishing characteristics. First, this series seeks to display exegetical accuracy. What the Bible says is what we want to say. While not every volume in the series will be a verse-by-verse commentary, we nevertheless desire to handle the text carefully and explain it rightly. Those who teach and preach bear the heavy responsibility of saying what God has said in His Word and declaring what God has done in Christ. We desire to handle God's Word faithfully, knowing that we must give an account for how we have fulfilled this holy calling (Jas 3:1).

Second, the Christ-Centered Exposition Commentary series has pastors in view. While we hope others will read this series, such as parents, teachers, small-group leaders, and student ministers, we desire to provide a commentary busy pastors will use for weekly preparation of biblically faithful and gospel-saturated sermons. This series is not academic in nature. Our aim is to present a readable and pastoral style of commentaries. We believe this aim will serve the church of the Lord Jesus Christ.

Third, we want the Christ-Centered Exposition Commentary series to be known for the inclusion of helpful illustrations and theologically driven applications. Many commentaries offer no help in illustrations, and few offer any kind of help in application. Often those that do offer illustrative material and application unfortunately give little serious attention to the text. While giving ourselves primarily to explanation, we also hope to serve readers by providing inspiring and illuminating illustrations coupled with timely and timeless application.

Finally, as the name suggests, the editors seek to exalt Jesus from every book of the Bible. In saying this, we are not commending wild allegory or fanciful typology. We certainly believe we must be constrained to the meaning intended by the divine Author Himself, the Holy Spirit of God. However, we also believe the Bible has a messianic focus, and our hope is that the individual authors will exalt Christ from particular texts. Luke 24:25-27,44-47 and John 5:39,46 inform both our hermeneutics and our homiletics. Not every author will do this the same way or have the same degree of Christ-centered emphasis. That is fine with us. We believe faithful exposition that is Christ centered is not monolithic. We do believe, however, that we must read the whole Bible as Christian Scripture. Therefore, our aim is both to honor the historical particularity of each biblical passage and to highlight its intrinsic connection to the Redeemer.

The editors are indebted to the contributors of each volume. The reader will detect a unique style from each writer, and we celebrate these unique gifts and traits. While distinctive in their approaches, the authors share a common characteristic in that they are pastoral theologians. They love the church, and they regularly preach and teach God's Word to God's people. Further, many of these contributors are younger voices. We think these new, fresh voices can serve the church well, especially among a rising generation that has the task of proclaiming the Word of Christ and the Christ of the Word to the lost world.

We hope and pray this series will serve the body of Christ well in these ways until our Savior returns in glory. If it does, we will have succeeded in our assignment.

David Platt
Daniel L. Akin
Tony Merida
Series Editors
February 2013

James

Faith Perseveres

JAMES 1:1-18

Main Idea: Trials and temptations are both inevitable, and God intends both to deepen our faith.

I. **Why James?**
   A. To examine the relationship between faith and works
   B. To explore the impact of our faith on
      1. life in this city
      2. life in this world
II. **Why Trials and Temptations?**
   A. God is sovereign over our trials (1:2-12).
      1. We learn to grow in His likeness.
      2. We learn to trust in His wisdom.
      3. We learn to rely on His resources.
      4. We learn to live for His reward.
   B. We are responsible in our temptations (1:13-15).
      1. The origin of sin
         a. God is perfectly sinless.
         b. We are utterly sinful.
      2. The anatomy of sin
         a. Step one: deception
         b. Step two: desire
         c. Step three: disobedience
         d. Step four: death
   C. God is faithful for our salvation (1:16-18).
      1. His goodness is unchanging.
      2. His goodness is undeserved.
      3. His goodness is unending.
         a. He has saved us from our sin.
         b. He will see us through our sorrow.

It's probably much easier to draw a crowd by preaching on the next and coolest topic that appeals to us, but what happens in the process is we start taking the parts of the Bible we like, tailoring it to what we want to hear, and creating a Christianity that appeals to us. We inevitably ignore the tough parts of the Bible, the parts of the Bible that confront us, the parts that cause us to change. Or we twist them out of context to fit our lifestyles.

The book of James is one of those tough and sometimes uncomfortable books. So why study James? Some background and context will be helpful in answering that question.

Why James?

The author of this book is most likely the James who was the half brother of Jesus. Acts 15 and 21 both indicate that James was the leader of the church in Jerusalem. James writes this book predominantly to Jewish Christians who were once associated with the church in Jerusalem. In God's providence, according to Acts 8, these Christians had been scattered when Stephen was martyred. This is why James opens the book, "James, a slave of God and of the Lord Jesus Christ," and then immediately begins to address the theme of trials and suffering.

There are two primary reasons to study the book of James. First, we study James **to examine the relationship between faith and works**. On the one hand, James refers to faith 14 different times in this letter. On the other hand, this letter from James is filled with commands to obey. Out of 108 verses, the book of James has 59 different commands (Doriani, *James*, 6). Obedience is everywhere. Genuine faith acts. Genuine faith works.

We live in a day when as soon as you talk about obedience, commands, laws, and the works of the Christian life, people cry, "Legalism!" and run away. People today say, "Christianity is not about doing this and this and this and this." Meanwhile, James says, "Yes it is!" You don't just listen to the Word; you do it. If you don't do it, your faith is dead—you don't even have faith (see 2:14-26). James might not make it as a pastor today since there might not be as many members at his church! Obviously we must be careful to understand the relationship between faith and works rightly and biblically, and this book challenges us. Nevertheless, the point of James is clear: there is a relationship between faith and works. It's immature, shallow, and (to be blunt) damning if you try to separate the two (see 5:1). This is serious stuff.

There's another aspect to the idea that faith works. Faith not only acts, but James also teaches us that faith is effective in the world. So the second reason we study James is **to explore the impact of our faith on life in this city and in this world.** James addresses many practical issues: trials, poverty, riches, materialism, favoritism, social justice, the tongue, worldliness, boasting, making plans, praying, and what to do when we're sick, among other things. As we'll see, James sometimes moves from one issue to the next, which can make it difficult to find the book's structure, but he returns repeatedly to how faith impacts not only the details of our lives but also the lives of people around us—both locally and globally. Faith moves Christians to lead Bible studies in workplaces and neighborhoods, help addicts in rehabilitation centers, serve food in homeless shelters, teach orphans in learning centers, care for widows in retirement homes, provide hospice care for the elderly, train men and women in job skills, tutor men and women in reading, rock sick babies in hospitals, help patients in AIDS clinics, teach English to internationals, and the list goes on and on. Faith moves Christians to take steps of radical obedience to make the gospel known all around the world.

Why Trials and Temptations?

James 1 introduces a variety of the book's themes, but its primary focus is trials and temptations. *Why* do we go through trials and face temptations? *How* do we go through trials and face temptations? The words *trials*, *tempt*, and *tempted* all occur in this section (1:2,12,13,14), and all of these words come from the same Greek word *peira*. This word can be translated as "trial" or "temptation." We'll see in the context of these verses why the word is translated both ways. As a whole, this important term will frame our understanding of James 1.

If I could summarize the main theme of verses 2-18 in one sentence, here is what it would be: "Trials and temptations are both inevitable, and God intends both to deepen our faith." Sometimes we face trials on the outside, and sometimes we face temptations on the inside, and how we understand them and respond to them has everything to do with our faith. So I want to highlight three truths that affect how we understand and respond to trials and temptations.

God Is Sovereign over Our Trials (1:2-12)

James tells us that trials are never out of God's control. Every trial we go through is under God's control, and He accomplishes His purposes through trials. Now, I'm guessing I'm not the only one who kind of wishes this passage wasn't in the Bible! Yet this is one of the most profound and crucial passages for mature, authentic Christian living. A blasphemous theology present today says God never wants you to be sick or poor, and you should name and claim health and wealth. James is writing to a hurting and predominantly poor community of Christians, and he is telling them to consider their trials "a great joy" (v. 2).

When James says to "consider it a great joy," this is a command, an imperative, and it's a verb that addresses how we think, which is important. This is not about feeling. Trials don't necessarily bring a smile to our faces. This is not simply about putting on a happy face and pretending everything is OK. In fact, I would go so far as to say that perhaps this should not always be the first thing out of your mouth when you are encouraging someone who is going through a trial. When life comes crashing down on someone, James doesn't intend for us to say flippantly, "Consider it joy, brother." I think about John 11, when Mary and Martha approached Jesus after their brother Lazarus had died. He didn't immediately start telling them that God had a purpose in this, although He knew God did. Instead, He comforted them and He wept with them (John 11:35).

So then, how do we experience pure joy when we experience a trial? Notice that James refers to "various trials" in verse 2. "Various" includes small trials, big trials, minor trials, and major trials. Sometimes we wonder why the little trials are there, and then when the big trials come, the tragedies and the difficulties that make the everyday trials seem so small, we wonder what James is thinking when he tells us to count all of these things as "great joy." How can the Bible be serious about this?

We need to realize that trials are not joyful in and of themselves, but they are joyful when we realize they are under the authority of a sovereign God who is accomplishing His purposes through them. And what is He accomplishing? In verses 3 and 4 James begins to pile on the ways God uses trials in our lives, and he continues all the way to verse 12 where he puts a bookend on this section by mentioning trials again. God is encouraging these believers to embrace trials not so much for what they are but for what God sovereignly accomplishes through them. We can learn at least four things in trials that should cause us to rejoice.

We learn to grow in His likeness. The testing of your faith develops "endurance" (v. 3), which must finish its work in you, so that you may be "mature and complete, lacking nothing" (v. 4). This is really the ultimate purpose for trials in this passage and in the book of James as a whole. God's goal in our lives is maturity in Him, growth in His likeness. One day every person is going to stand before Almighty God, and God's goal from now until then is to prepare you for that day. We don't think like this, for we think the goal of life is to be successful, to have a nice job, to get a raise, to achieve a standing in the world, to attain a certain goal, or to have a certain kind of family. Then when trials hit in our family, at work, or with some plans we have, they devastate us. But if our goal is to know God and to be conformed into His likeness, then we can take joy in trials because we can know that no matter how tough these trials are, they are moving us toward our goal.

A James 1:3 kind of lifestyle, the kind that endures because of testing, requires a radically God-centered perspective on life. Think of a trial in your own life (whether it's big or small): if the goal is just to fix your circumstances, then you are setting yourself up for constant frustration because often the circumstance won't get fixed like you want it to, and sometimes it won't get fixed at all. Even when it is fixed like you want it, something else will come up. You will live in constant anxiety. But if your ultimate goal is not just to fix your circumstances but to know God and to grow in God, then rejoice because no matter what your circumstances, you will achieve your goal. God has designed trials for your growth in godliness. Trials are joy when God is our goal. I love what Malcolm Muggeridge said on this topic:

> Contrary to what might be expected, I look back on experiences that at the time seemed especially desolating and painful with particular satisfaction. Indeed, I can say with complete truthfulness that everything I have learned in my seventy-five years in this world, everything that has truly enhanced and enlightened my existence, has been through affliction and not through happiness, whether pursued or attained. (Muggeridge, *Tesimony*, n.p.)

In trials we experience growth in godliness like we could never experience any other way. This is not encouraging if your goal is to have a nice, easy, carefree life—your best life, as it's called—with all the circumstances going like you have planned. If that's your goal, then trials will never be a joy to you. But when you set your sights above the stuff of this world and you fix your eyes on God and the knowledge of Him and maturity in Him, then trials will be a joy to you because they will teach you to know, love, and trust Him.

We learn to trust in His wisdom. The implication in verse 5 is clear: We're not there yet when it comes to wisdom. We are lacking something, and that something is wisdom, which is what we need when we walk through trials. Like verse 2, verse 5 gives an imperative: "He should ask God." This is what we are to do when we lack wisdom. In relation to the wisdom of God, our own wisdom grows through three different factors: knowledge, perspective, and experience. Our limitations in all three of these areas lead to limited wisdom. When we walk through trials, we realize we don't know all that is going on (knowledge); we don't see our situation from every angle (perspective); we oftentimes lack experience in what to do (experience). God, on the other hand, possesses all knowledge, He has an eternal perspective, and in Christ He has experienced every kind of test and has prevailed. And we can ask God because He "gives to all generously and without criticizing" (v. 5).

Verse 5 has to be one of the most beautiful and encouraging promises in all of Scripture. God gives wisdom generously, abundantly, liberally. He pours it out to all without discrimination, without question, and without hesitation. This is the God of the universe saying, "I will impart My wisdom to you." But it's not automatic. You must ask for it. And God doesn't give us the easy answer. When we are in a trial, we just want our circumstances fixed. But God says, "Draw near to Me, and ask Me to help you understand why this is happening and to give you perspective on what you are going through and to walk alongside you as the One who possesses all knowledge, eternal perspective, and perfect experience."

My father was the wisest man I have ever known. He died unexpectedly in 2004, and I would give anything to have one more conversation with him. I'm confident that conversation would be long because I've got a lot to learn in life. I would love to pepper him with questions, then just sit back and listen. But I have something infinitely better: the sovereign King of creation has made His wisdom available to me and to all followers of Christ. So when you go through trials, ask God to give you wisdom and trust Him to give it to you. James tells us not to doubt (v. 6), and this holds true even when life is not easy or doesn't make sense. Believe that God is wise and that He is with you.

Consider an example from your personal experience with other people. If you share life with someone and you see the wise decisions they make as they go through hard times, then you will naturally grow to trust that person the next time a trial comes. This is God's design in our relationship with Him, and He is right every time, so the more we walk through trials with Him, the more we will learn to trust in Him. *We learn to rely on His resources.* Verses 9-11 introduce the theme of riches and poverty that we see throughout James. But why, in the middle of this section on trials, does James start talking about poverty and riches? Many of James's readers were likely poor, but some were rich and were trusting in their wealth. James reminds us in these verses that trials have a remarkable leveling effect. If you are poor, you should boast in the fact that your circumstances are actually leading you to trust in God; and in the absence of physical resources, you are driven to boast in your (paradoxically) rich status as a child of God. On the other hand, if you are rich, be careful. Trials will remind you that money can't solve your problems, and all of the stuff you fill your life with can't cover up your hurts. One day all that stuff is going to be burned in the fire, and you're going to have nothing left. Will your life be built on those physical resources or on the spiritual resources only God can provide?

We learn to live for His reward. James closes this section in verse 12 by saying the man who endures trials is "blessed," which is just one of many examples in the book of James where he deliberately alludes to the Sermon on the Mount. The key to understanding this whole book is realizing that James is leaning heavily on Jesus' teachings in the Sermon on the Mount. When James talks about the "crown of life" that the man who endures will receive, there are two ways to misunderstand this image. First, don't picture some "gem-studded headpiece worn by kings or queens": most original readers of this letter would have heard this word and immediately thought about the wreath that would be put on an athlete's head at the end of a race he won (Moo, *James*, 70). The picture here is that of running through the trials of this life victoriously to receive this crown. Second, the crown of life should not simply be thought of as a physical crown with great splendor. No, the crown is actually a symbol of receiving the glorious reward of eternal life. At the end of these trials, God meets us with life, eternal life. So consider it joy because trials remind you that you are living for a reward to come. Paul puts it this way in 2 Corinthians 4:17: "For our momentary light affliction is producing for us an absolutely incomparable eternal weight of glory."

We Are Responsible in Our Temptations (1:13-15)

The first truth we've seen is that God is sovereign in our trials; consequently, our trials can be a joy. But James wants to protect us against something here, which he explains in the second major truth in this passage. God, in His sovereignty, will test the faith of His people, and He will do it for our good. This truth can be found all over Scripture (see, for example, Rom 8:28; Heb 12:5-6). But we have to be careful not to take the next step in our minds and begin to assume that God tempts us to turn from Him. This is such a slippery slope.

Every trial brings temptation with it. When we face financial difficulty, we are tempted to distrust God's provision. When someone dear to us dies, we are tempted to question God's love. When we experience unjust suffering, we are tempted to impugn God's justice. But know this: God may test us, but according to verse 13, He does not and cannot and will not tempt us. We are responsible in temptations.

The origin of sin. Understanding who is responsible in temptation requires understanding the origin of sin. James says clearly in verse 13 that **God is perfectly sinless**. Everything in Him resists sin; evil is inherently foreign to Him. He is aware of it, but He is untainted by it. In no way can God be blamed for temptation and sin. Who is responsible then?

To answer that question, James holds up the mirror and says, "But each person is tempted when he is drawn away and enticed by his own evil desires" (v. 14). God is perfectly sinless, but **we are utterly sinful**. After telling us God does not tempt us to sin, we might expect James to say Satan drags us away and entices us, but he doesn't. Now, that doesn't mean Satan isn't involved in the temptations of this world; this will become clear later in this book (4:7). However, the responsibility for temptation and sin lies squarely with us, for our sinful desires within lead us to give in to temptation. We have no one else to blame for our sin.

May God help us understand this in a world where there are efforts at every turn to absolve us from our responsibility for sin. We want to put the fault on others or blame our upbringing, our friends, our family, our government, our condition, or anything else we can think of. This doesn't mean different factors don't affect us all in different ways, but the teaching of Scripture is clear: the fault for my sin lies with me. There is a problem at the core of who you are and who I am. In the words of Paul in Romans 7:18, "For I know that nothing good lives in me, that is, in my flesh."

The anatomy of sin. Having looked at the origin of sin, we also need to consider the anatomy of sin. Sin does not just happen out of the blue.

There is a process behind it, and we might think about this in the following four steps:

1. **Deception.** Genesis 3 presents a perfect example of this process with Adam and Eve. The heart of sin is unbelief—not believing God. We don't believe God when He says something is best for us or another thing is not. Instead, we question Him. This is where sin starts, and we see it in the serpent's question, "Did God really say, 'You can't eat from any tree in the garden?'" (Gen 3:1).

2. **Desire.** James says each one is tempted when he is "drawn away and enticed by his own evil desires" (v. 14). The language here carries the idea of baiting a hook. No fish knowingly bites an empty hook. The idea is to hide the hook. Temptation appeals to our desires, attracts us, but hides the fact that it will kill us. This kind of desire drives men to pornography, women into another man's arms, employees to dishonesty, and people to a number of other sins. Sin starts with disordered thought, which leads to disordered desire, and we begin to want that which will destroy us. When we are enticed and when desire like that is conceived, it gives birth to sin.

3. **Disobedience.** We act on our desire.

4. **Death.** This is the result of disobedience. The imagery of death is vivid and terrifying, and we need to see it for the horror it is.

Brother or sister in Christ, whatever sin you are flirting with, whatever deception you are buying or desires you are fulfilling, run away from them. They will kill you. And this is *in* us!

God Is Faithful for Our Salvation (1:16-18)

So, what do we do during trials and temptations, the very time when we are so prone to fix our eyes on our circumstances that we miss what God has in store? What do we do in the midst of temptations, when we are so prone to be dragged away and enticed by the desires that are at the core of our lives? We remember that God is faithful for our salvation. With God, James tells us in 1:17, "there is no variation or shadow cast by turning." In your trials or temptations, don't believe the lies. Remember that God is good, so very good. And He wants that which is good for you. So trust Him in your trials, and turn to Him in your temptations. He is the source of everything good (v. 17). Simply consider these three different aspects of God's goodness.

His goodness is unchanging. God is perpetually, constantly, consistently good. He never gets in a bad mood. He never changes for the worse, and He never changes for the better because He is already perfectly and ultimately and wonderfully good in every way, and you can't get any better than God. If He could change for the better, that would mean He wasn't ultimately good in the first place, but He is.

His goodness is undeserved. Verse 18 says that God chose to give us birth through the "message of truth." We're going to see a lot about works in James, but the foundation is all about grace. God has given us new life based not on our works but on His grace. He chose to give us birth! He chose to take His Word and write it on our hearts, hearts that were sinful to the core. This is the gospel, the message of Christianity—anything good in you is because of God's undeserved goodness toward you! God is the source of every good thing in us. Were it not for Him, everything in us would be bad. We need His undeserved goodness to change us from the inside out. This is what faith relies on at every level.

His goodness is unending. We are the "firstfruits of His creatures" (v. 18). The picture of firstfruits carries the idea of a foretaste of that which is to come. What God has done in our lives to change our hearts by His goodness is only a preview of the day to come when He will make all things new in all creation. And the work He has done in our new birth will one day lead to a new heaven and a new earth where there will be no more trials and no more temptations.

In the meantime, take heart, Christian. **He has saved us from our sin.** And if He has saved us from our sin, then we can know beyond the shadow of a doubt that **He will see us through our sorrow.** Contemplate the truth of this gospel, of a God who conquers sin and suffering through the death and resurrection of Jesus Christ so that today you and I can consider trials pure joy and face temptations with steadfast confidence.

Reflect and Discuss

1. How do unbelievers you know attempt to make it through painful circumstances? How have you persevered through such times in your life?
2. What qualifies as a trial? What about a temptation? How do trials test the genuineness of your faith?
3. If true faith endures to the end, how is this not a way of earning your salvation?
4. How should the need to persevere in faith affect the way we counsel those who have just recently professed Christ?
5. Explain how believing in God's sovereignty through our trials is crucial to persevering faith.
6. List some ways painful circumstances and unanswered questions can actually strengthen your faith.
7. Since God is sovereign, does this mean we are not at fault when we give in to sin? Explain your answer.
8. How does Scripture counsel us to overcome sin's attractions?
9. If someone no longer has an interest in being a Christian due to a trial, what should we conclude about that person's faith? How would you counsel that person?
10. What role does knowing our final reward play in enduring trials?

Faith Obeys

JAMES 1:19-25

Main Idea: Followers of Christ should receive God's Word humbly, remember it constantly, and obey it wholeheartedly.

The Journey of Obedience

I.   **We Receive the Word Humbly (1:19-21).**

II. **We Remember the Word Constantly (1:22-25).**

III. **We Obey the Word Wholeheartedly (1:22).**

Some things in Scripture are prescriptive. Scripture is prescribing how we should live. Scripture is giving us commands that, by the grace of God, we should and must obey for the good of our lives and for the glory of God.

But then there are times when Scripture includes events that are descriptive. In other words Scripture describes something that happens. Now, it's important in those instances when the Word is *describing* an event not immediately to assume that this means Scripture is *prescribing* something. For example, when Balaam has a conversation one day with a donkey (Num 22:28-30), Scripture is describing this event, but Scripture is not prescribing that God's people should talk to donkeys. This is not a command that we should obey.

In that light I would like to *describe* something God has done in my life and family that I would not necessarily *prescribe* (or suggest that God *prescribes*) for others. But I share this part of my own spiritual journey to shed light on how James 1:19-25 has affected my life personally.

Not long ago God began convicting me about how I was using the resources He has entrusted to me. God used chapters like 2 Corinthians 8–9 and 1 Timothy 6 to uncover a lack of priority for the poor in my life. The more I studied Scripture, the more I realized how important the poor are to God. The more I looked at my life, the more I realized how indifferent I was toward the poor.

In 2005, Hurricane Katrina invaded my life and family, sending our house underwater and causing us to lose pretty much everything we had. As a result, we had a chance to start over with nothing and acquire possessions more simply and wisely in this world. In a world that says, "You need more and bigger and better," this was our chance to start over and not live according to that mantra. But we blew it. Within a year after Katrina, we had moved to Birmingham, Alabama, and we had more stuff than we ever had before. We bought a big house, and if you have a big house, you've got to fill it with something, so we bought furniture to fill the house, and things were going smoothly until God's Spirit through God's Word began to convict my heart as I asked the question, "Why? Why am I spending so much on myself when God has spoken so clearly, commanding me to give generously, sacrificially, and cheerfully of my resources for others?"

Unfortunately, I ignored the Word of God. I put God off. Yet, by His grace, He walked with me in my disobedience until finally His Word broke through my hard heart, and I realized, "We need to make some changes."

So I went to Heather, my precious wife, and I shared various Scriptures with her, and I told her I believed we needed to sell our house and move into a smaller one in order to free up our resources for God's purposes in order to align our lives more with God's Word. We started praying together about it that night, and within a month there was a for-sale sign in our yard. Thus began the journey of trying to sell our house in a time when the housing market was collapsing. We had bought at the height of the housing market, and now we were selling at its nadir. As a result, I was constantly pulled to ask, "Is this wise? Is this good?" We had started the process of adoption again, and some days we thought to ourselves, "Should we really be making this change? Our family is growing, so isn't it contradictory to downsize your house when you're family is upsizing?" Meanwhile, we would have different little things go wrong with the house while it was for sale that needed to be fixed, and we would think, "Why are we spending money on a house we're selling?" To make matters worse, every time a plumber or an electrician or whoever would come over to the house, their inevitable first words were, "This is such a great house. Why are you selling it?"

That year of working to sell our house was filled with ups and downs, questions and struggles, opportunities that came and went. But in the middle of it all, even in the middle of our questions, we knew this was what the Lord was leading us to do. He had spoken clearly in His Word about our priorities, and this was the way we sensed He was calling us to put that Word into practice.

I could go on to talk about all the ways God provided for us as we made this change in our lives, including how and where He led us in ways we never could have imagined. In the same way, I could go on to talk about the many other areas of my life that God is still refining to align with His Word. But the clear lesson my precious wife and I learned together in this process was that we never want to rest content simply to hear the Word of God and not act on it. We don't want to put God off. Even when it's challenging, we want to obey God, no matter what, knowing that obedience to God in His Word is more important than anything else in this world.

The Journey of Obedience

This journey of obedience is what James 1:19-25 is all about. The Word of God is all over this passage. It's referenced in verses 21,22,23, and 25, not to mention verse 18 from the previous section. In verses 1-18 we tried to answer the question, How do we respond to trials? Now the question in this section is, How do we respond to truth—the truth of God's Word? Based on James 1:19-25, there are three ways we respond to the Word.

We Receive the Word Humbly
JAMES 1:19-21

In verse 19 James says we are to be "quick to hear." Basically, he's saying, "Hurry up and listen" (Blomberg and Kamell, *James*, 85). James also tells us to be quiet, or "slow to speak." Be humble as you approach the Word, not coming with your defenses up, which leads to anger and resistance to the Word. Don't we often approach God's Word talking and not listening? Don't we often come to God's Word thinking, "Here's what I want it to say"? Don't we often come to God's Word looking to justify ourselves? We're like people in an argument who are not really listening to one another, but instead we're consumed with formulating what we're going to say in response. We are not quick to hear and slow to speak but loathe to listen and anxious to argue. We hear a verse like Luke 12:33, "Sell your possessions and give to the poor," and we're already thinking, "How do I get around that?" And this has been true of

God's people throughout history. Instead of humbly listening to God's Word, His people have resisted it. This was the response of God's people to the prophets in the Old Testament who proclaimed His Word, to Jesus when He spoke the words of the Father, and to Paul after he preached in the synagogues. The crowds in Lystra stoned Paul and dragged him out of town at the instigation of unbelieving Jews (Acts 14:19). Seeing what happened in Scripture to people who proclaimed God's Word will come close to talking you out of being a preacher. Those who proclaim the Word of God don't often end up well in the world.

James says to the people of God, "Be quick to hear" (v. 19). Then in verse 21 he tells them to get rid of "all moral filth and evil." The word translated "ridding yourselves" literally carries the idea of taking off a garment. We bring so many ideas from the world that the Word confronts and counters. The Word thinks so much differently from the world! James tells us to put aside the sinful and selfish ideas of the world and to come humbly to the Word. When I read passages in a book like James about the poor and the way we spend our resources, I think, "How do we get around this?" And then I'm reminded that the goal is never to get around God's Word. Why would you want to get around it?

The second part of verse 21 gives us really good news as James talks about the Word that is planted in you. We need to understand Jeremiah 31 to grasp what James is referring to when he talks about the "implanted word." Jeremiah the prophet was speaking to a people who were not living up to God's law. In fact, they *couldn't* keep it. And Jeremiah gives them this promise, the promise of the new covenant:

> *"Look, the days are coming"—this is the LORD's declaration—"when I will make a new covenant with the house of Israel and with the house of Judah. This one will not be like the covenant I made with their ancestors when I took them by the hand to bring them out of the land of Egypt—a covenant they broke even though I had married them"—the LORD's declaration. "Instead, this is the covenant I will make with the house of Israel after those days"—the LORD's declaration. "I will put My teaching within them and write it on their hearts. I will be their God, and they will be My people.* (Jer 31:31-33)

According to Jeremiah's prophecy, God was going to write His law on the hearts of His people, or plant it in their hearts, to use James's language. Ezekiel 36 says the same thing with beautiful imagery:

For I will take you from the nations and gather you from all the
countries, and will bring you into your own land. I will also sprinkle
clean water on you, and you will be clean. I will cleanse you from all
your impurities and all your idols. I will give you a new heart and
put a new spirit within you; I will remove your heart of stone and
give you a heart of flesh. I will place My Spirit within you and cause
you to follow My statutes and carefully observe My ordinances. (Ezek
36:24-27)

God puts His law on our hearts (Jer 31) and His Spirit in our hearts
(Ezek 36), and the Spirit of God though the Word of God moves us.
This is the language of James 1 (18,21). God has planted His Word in
us, and our hearts find life in this Word. Like the blood that flows to our
hearts, we need this Word.

May God help us in our day, for we need this Word that is able to
save us. The language here is potent, emphasizing how we are not saved
by working but by receiving the Word, and how that Word planted in us
then moves us to action. This is the heart of James. We work and put our
faith into action, yes, but we do this by the Word at work in our hearts,
the Word that has given us life (v. 18). As you accept this Word and humbly submit to it, your soul experiences the depths of salvation. Don't
underestimate the power and the importance of the Word of God.

Do you long to receive this Word? If you do, that is good. It should
be a treasured and cherished possession for you. If it is not, then get
rid of the filth and evil and worldliness that are drawing your affections
away from the Word that saves you. Receive the Word humbly.

We Remember the Word Constantly
JAMES 1:22-25

This point is closely intertwined with the response of humility in verses
19-21. In verse 25 James talks about the man who "looks intently into
the perfect law of freedom." The phrase "looks intently" can be used to
refer to stooping down and looking closely at something (Moo, *James*,
93). It's like when my three-year-old son sees a bug, and he stops in his
tracks and bends down to put his face inches from the ground to look
at it. He gazes on it. Likewise, amid the busyness of our lives, we need to
stop for some time during the day, look at the Word, read it, and study it.
Don't be content with a little word from God for the day. Dive in deep.

The language here carries the idea of looking "with penetrating absorption." Absorb the Word.
     The man who absorbs the perfect law that gives freedom and continues to do so will not forget what he hears. In verses 23-24 James contrasts this kind of man with another man who doesn't remember the Word. James uses a deliberately ridiculous analogy of a person who gazes into his own face in a mirror but then seconds later couldn't even pick himself out of a police lineup. He forgets what he looked like. James says not to do this with the Word—don't forget it.
     This command not to forget God's Word reminds us of the history of God's people. In Deuteronomy God gave His people His law, the second giving of the law, before the people went into the promised land.[1] Deuteronomy 6:4-9 contains one of the most important passages in Israel's history, and it relates to remembering God's Word:

> Listen, Israel: The LORD our God, the LORD is One. Love the LORD your God with all your heart, with all your soul, and with all your strength. These words that I am giving you today are to be in your heart. Repeat them to your children. Talk about them when you sit in your house and when you walk along the road, when you lie down and when you get up. Bind them as a sign on your hand and let them be a symbol on your forehead. Write them on the doorposts of your house and on your gates.

A couple of chapters later in Deuteronomy, we see God warning His people not to forget His commands and decrees:

> When you eat and are full, you will praise the LORD your God for the good land He has given you.
>   Be careful that you don't forget the LORD your God by failing to keep His command—the ordinances and statutes—I am giving you today. When you eat and are full, and build beautiful houses to live in, and your herds and flocks grow large, and your silver and gold multiply, and everything else you have increases, be careful that your heart doesn't become proud and you forget the LORD your God who brought you out of the land of Egypt, out of the place of slavery. He led you through the great and terrible wilderness with its poisonous snakes

---

[1] The title "Deuteronomy" means "second law" or "repetition of the law."

and scorpions, a thirsty land where there was no water. He brought water out of the flint-like rock for you. He fed you in the wilderness with manna that your fathers had not known, in order to humble and test you, so that in the end He might cause you to prosper. You may say to yourself, "My power and my own ability have gained this wealth for me," but remember that the LORD *your God gives you the power to gain wealth, in order to confirm His covenant He swore to your fathers, as it is today.* (Deut 8:10-18)

Don't forget God's Word: let it lodge in your heart and in your mind; have it always before you. The importance of God's Word is one reason I believe memorization of Scripture is an all-important spiritual discipline for every Christian. People say, "I can't memorize Scripture," and I want to be careful because I know that believers have different abilities to memorize. At the same time, Psalm 19 says the Word is more precious than gold, than "an abundance of pure gold" (Ps 19:10). The question is, "Do we value Scripture?" Do we value it more than we value our reality TV shows, the songs we download on iTunes, and the stats of our favorite sports teams? We tend to commit to memory those things we value most.

If all we do is listen to the Word when we come together for corporate worship, then we are like this fool in James 1:23-24. We listen and leave, and then by lunch, or perhaps by dinner, it's all gone. What good is that? This is why, in my own church, we have intentionally set up encouragement to memorize Scripture so that every week there is a verse (most of the time from the passage we are studying) to memorize. Men ought to lead their families to memorize Scripture together. Singles ought to memorize Scripture together. In a variety of ways and in the context of a variety of relationships, we ought to be encouraging one another to hide this Word in our hearts. If we don't, we will open God's Word and see sin for the horrible evil that it is, and then we will see God's gracious provision in Christ, but we will depart and go on our way as if we had never been exposed to these realities. This is not just dangerous; it's damning.

We Obey the Word Wholeheartedly
JAMES 1:22

So far in our response to the Word, we've seen that we are to receive the Word humbly and remember the Word constantly. Third and finally, we obey the Word wholeheartedly. James 1:22 is the theme verse of the entire book of James. It says, "But be doers of the word and not hearers only, deceiving yourselves." You have not really listened to the Word if you have not obeyed the Word. The bottom line is that the Word evokes action, and if there is no action from the Word, then clearly there has been no acceptance of the Word. This is the essence of faith. James 2 describes saving faith in more depth, but even here in chapter 1 we see this reality: those who have accepted Jesus obey Jesus. To think any differently is to live in deception. To say, "I have accepted Jesus," but then to live contrary to Jesus is to deceive oneself (1 John 2:4). James says you are blind to your true spiritual condition if you claim to have heard and received and accepted this word, yet you fail to act on it. You are deceiving yourself, for you think you're right with God because you listened to the Word, maybe even because you listened intently. But according to James, you're wrong.

James's words sound eerily familiar to Jesus' words in the Sermon on the Mount:

> *Not everyone who says to Me, "Lord, Lord!" will enter the kingdom of*
> *heaven, but only the one who does the will of My Father in heaven. On*
> *that day many will say to Me, "Lord, Lord, didn't we prophesy in Your*
> *name, drive out demons in Your name, and do many miracles in Your*
> *name?" Then I will announce to them, "I never knew you! Depart*
> *from Me, you lawbreakers!"*
>
> *Therefore, everyone who hears these words of Mine and acts*
> *on them will be like a sensible man who built his house on the rock.*
> *The rain fell, the rivers rose, and the winds blew and pounded that*
> *house. Yet it didn't collapse, because its foundation was on the rock.*
> *But everyone who hears these words of Mine and doesn't act on them*
> *will be like a foolish man who built his house on the sand. The rain*
> *fell, the rivers rose, the winds blew and pounded that house, and it*
> *collapsed. And its collapse was great!* (Matt 7:21-27)

If your spiritual life is built on merely listening to the words of Jesus and not on obeying them, then one day your life will eternally and ultimately end in destruction. And the danger is that you're going to think you're OK all the way up until that day. Bishop Brownrig said, "To deceive is bad, to deceive yourselves is worse, to deceive yourselves about your souls is worst of all" (in Spurgeon, "Before Sermon"). I am frighteningly convinced that countless people within the church listen to the Word

week by week, and yet it is not planted in their heart, and it is evident
because they are not acting on it. Sure, they act on the things that agree
with their lifestyle, or they act when it is convenient to obey. But when
this Word confronts, challenges, convicts, or tries to change them, they
put it aside and forget it, never putting it into action. Be careful if this
describes your life because this is not the Christian life. In the Christian
life the Word is planted in your heart, and you receive it like blood to
your heart, humbly and constantly, and by the grace of God that moves
your heart, you obey it. This is the Christian life. A life that is doing what
this Word says.

As a pastor, one of the phrases that most concerns me is when someone says, "I just need to be willing to obey God's Word, particularly when
it calls me to do something radical in my life or my culture. I just need
to be willing. That's enough." Based on James 1, I want to warn you that
this mind-set is extremely deceptive. Now, there's a grain of truth here,
for Psalm 51:17 says, "You will not despise a broken and humbled heart."
God desires a willing heart, just as God desires a listening heart, a heart
that trembles at His Word (Isa 66). But if you listen and you don't do
anything, you've not really listened. And if you're willing, but you don't
do anything, you're not really willing.

Don't be *willing* to obey the Word; obey the Word. Don't be *willing*
to help the poor; help the poor. Don't be *willing* to share the gospel;
share the gospel. Don't be *willing* to live in purity; live in purity. We are
to "be doers of the word and not hearers only" (v. 22). This exhorta-
tion—do it—can sound burdensome if we're not careful. However, listen to the language in James 1:25:

> But the one who looks intently into the perfect law of freedom and
> perseveres in it, and is not a forgetful hearer but one who does good
> works—this person will be blessed in what he does.

James switches from speaking of the "word" to describing "the perfect
law of freedom." As soon as you start talking about obeying God's Word
or His law today, many people hear that as legalistic, and they run away.
But James says not to run, for the law is good. The "perfect law" James
refers to in verse 25 is not the Old Testament law of Moses but rather
the law understood through Christ—that is, the words of Christ and
the truth of Christ that free us from slavery to sin and this world. The
law says to us, "There is another way." Look at this way, this law, and do
it, and you will be "blessed" in what you do (v. 25). It sounds like that

blessing is conditional, and if you're wondering whether you have to do something in order to experience blessing, no, I'm not saying that—James is! And it's not just James—it's Jesus too, along with the rest of Scripture![2]

We have created a Christianity that stops at saying Jesus loves you just the way you are and Jesus loves you no matter what you do. Certainly, there's glorious truth to this when it comes to Jesus saving us from our sins, no matter how horrible they are, and Jesus loving us when we have nothing in us to deserve such love. But at the same time, Jesus says things like, "You are My friends if you do what I command you" (John 15:14). And, "If anyone loves Me, he will keep My word" (John 14:23). John tells us in 1 John 2:4, "The one who says, 'I have come to know Him [Jesus],' yet doesn't keep His commands, is a liar, and the truth is not in him." So, how do we understand all this? How do we understand a law that brings freedom *and* an obedience that God commands? Understanding this concept helps bring the whole passage together.

James tells us glorious blessing is to be experienced in obedience to God's Word. That naturally leads us to wonder, "How do you obey God's Word?" The answer is not that you muster up obedience to the best of your ability. No, the answer is to receive the Word humbly, the Word planted in you, and to focus on it, remember it, and hide it in your heart and on your mind. As you do this, that Word which initially gave you life as a Christian will work in and through you and move you to follow God's decrees.

So don't settle for just listening to it. There are surely many followers of Christ to whom God has been speaking for days, weeks, months, maybe even years, and by His Word He's been calling them to do something in particular in their life or in their family. My counsel is this: Do it. Receive the Word humbly, remember it constantly, and obey it wholeheartedly.

For some followers of Christ, there may be an area of outright disobedience or an area of delayed obedience. It's an area of life where they have been putting off God's Word. They know what God's Word says, but they are not putting it into practice. The Word is saying, "Care for the poor," and yet they're still not doing it. The Word is saying, "Turn from gossip, turn from pornography, be reconciled to your spouse," and they are ignoring it because it doesn't fit with what they want. Or maybe

---

[2] See for example Matt 24:45-51; Luke 11:28; 1 Pet 3:9; Rev 22:7.

the Word is saying something that so goes against the grain of the way this culture works, and they think, "I don't know if anybody will understand." In the end we must obey God's Word, regardless of the circumstances or consequences. This is one of the marks of true faith as the Bible defines it.

One of the books that has had an impact on me when it comes to the house church in China is called *Back to Jerusalem*. It is written by three Chinese pastors, and at the end of the book the pastors talk about the difference between believers and disciples, that is, people who just say they believe in Christ and people who are really following Christ. I think that difference is akin to James's distinction between hearers and doers. These pastors write, "True disciples are usually people that few understand. They are viewed as potentially unstable fanatics. Often the same governments that tolerate the existence of mere believers will stop at no ends to completely eradicate any disciples within their borders" (Yun, Yongze, and Wang, *Back to Jerusalem*, 115). Did you catch that? These pastors are saying that the government in China really does not care about people who are listening to the Word. But the government wants to imprison people who are doing the Word.

We stall so often at this point, and I want to be careful because I'm not suggesting that we throw godly, biblical counsel out the window and act without thinking. But at the same time, we can so worry ourselves by thinking that we might mess up that we end up not doing anything at all. If you are listening to the Word and absorbing yourself in it, I want to encourage you that you can rest confident that the Word planted in your heart is going to lead and guide you. So abide in God, abide in His Word, and when He speaks, obey.

Reflect and Discuss

1. What role should God's Word play in our pursuit of Christlikeness?
2. Why do you think so many professing Christians struggle to find time for God's Word? Is it a problem of discipline or desire? Or both?
3. What does it say about our hearts that we often find it difficult to listen instead of expressing our opinion?
4. How does a heart bent on sin affect the way we receive God's Word? How have you seen this play out in your own life?
5. Explain this statement: the Word that requires obedience empowers obedience.

6. Outside of corporate worship, how does Scripture influence the way you think and live? What are some specific ways you could grow in this area?

7. Why is it deceptive to hear God's Word and not obey it?

8. Can you think of people you know who profess to follow Christ but show no evidence of being saved? How might you approach them with wisdom and boldness?

9. List some areas of your life where you've said you're willing to obey, but you're not actively obeying. How will you move forward in these areas?

10. How is James's call for obedience different from an attempt to earn a right standing before God—that is, works-righteousness?

Faith Loves

Main Idea: True and acceptable religion must include controlled speech, sacrificial care for the needy, and clear separation from the world, all as a manifestation of faith expressing itself through love.

I. **The Marks of True and Acceptable Religion**
   A. Controlled speech that displays a changed heart (1:26)
   B. Sacrificial care for those in need (1:27)
      1. They are helpless.
      2. We must be selfless.
   C. Clear separation from the ways of the world (1:27–2:13)
      1. We are captivated by the glory of Christ.
      2. We are gripped by the grace of Christ.
      3. We are devoted to the law of Christ.
      4. We are cognizant of the judgment of Christ.
      5. We are a reflection of the mercy of Christ.

II. **The Manifestation of True and Acceptable Religion**

Søren Kierkegaard, Danish philosopher and theologian, once said, "The human race in the course of time has taken the liberty of softening and softening Christianity until at last we have contrived to make it exactly the opposite of what it is in the New Testament" (*Attack*, 39).

I agree with Kierkegaard in that we try at every turn to define Christianity on our terms instead of on the terms of God outlined in the New Testament. I am convinced the deep, dark secret of our religious subculture in the southern United States is that we want Christianity and we want church on our terms, according to our preferences, aligning with our lifestyles. We are a people happy to go to church just so long as nothing in our lives has to change. We are a people glad to be Christians just so long as we can define Christianity according to what accommodates us. The only problem is that in order for the religion of Christianity to be authentic, true, and actually acceptable before God, we have to let Him define what it looks like. And His definition of religion, His definition of true Christianity, is radically different from ours.

In this section of James, we are going to see a New Testament explanation of faith and religion—the kind of religion that honors and is acceptable to God—and we are going to be faced with a choice. Are we going to define religion on our terms and settle for a Christianity that appeals to our lifestyles? Or are we going to submit to God's terms for what faith, religion, and Christianity look like in our lives, in our families, and in our churches? Be careful how you answer. Martin Luther said, "A religion that gives nothing, costs nothing, and suffers nothing, is worth nothing." James 1–2 may turn your idea of Christianity upside down.

The Marks of True and Acceptable Religion

The word *religion* doesn't have a positive connotation in many circles, and it really isn't used all that often in the New Testament. But James is introducing a section here where he's going to show us that true religion is characterized by a lifestyle of obedience to God. In the last two verses of chapter 1, he gives us a picture of three marks of true and acceptable religion, and then he expands on the third mark in chapter 2. We need to think about our lives and our faith in terms of these three marks.

Controlled Speech That Displays a Changed Heart (1:26)

The first mark of true and acceptable religion is controlled speech that displays a changed heart. James makes this point in 1:26, one of many times he talks about our speech (see especially 3:1-12). Keep in mind that James leans heavily on what Jesus taught in the Gospels. Jesus clearly taught that what we speak is a reflection of what is in our heart: "For the mouth speaks from the overflow of the heart" (Matt 12:34; see also Matt 15:18; Luke 6:45). Our speech is a reflection of what is inside of us such that if our speech is not controlled, James says our religion is a sham—worthless, vain, and meaningless.

Oh, Christian brother or sister, be warned here! Don't deceive yourself: when you speak, you tell the truth about your heart. The way men speak to and about their wives tells the truth about their hearts. Likewise, the way women speak to and about their husbands tells the truth about their hearts. The way you speak to your friends, the way you speak to your family, the way you speak about others—all of these things are indicators of whether or not your faith is real. If you are engaging in gossip, if your words are biting, if they are cursing, if they are angry, even if they are just plain inundated with trivialities, then be careful; you are showing that your religion is worthless.

James is saying that **the tongue is the test of true religion**. I want to be careful here because the tongue—what we say—is not the only indicator of our hearts. And we can oftentimes make professions with our lips that are not backed up by our lives. But I believe there is a word of application here for us. In a day of text-messaging, e-mail, cell phones, Twitter, blogs, Facebook, etc., we need to be careful. We've created an entire culture that says if you have a thought, then you should immediately share it with the rest of the world. But follower of Christ, don't buy that line of thinking. Keep a tight rein on your tongue, and speak in a way that shows your faith is real and the core of your heart belongs to God.

Sacrificial Care for Those in Need (1:27)

Next James says, "Pure and undefiled religion before our God and Father is this: to look after orphans and widows in their distress and to keep oneself unstained by the world." Here we see both practical compassion and personal purity. Whether in religion or in politics, we often avoid one of these. In politics we can jump on a right-wing, conservative platform and talk about how we need to protect our morals and the sanctity of marriage and life. Or we can jump on a left-wing, liberal platform and talk about how we need to be concerned socially about the poor, the weak, the downcast, and the oppressed. And James says yes to both. Now, I'm not saying James was a Republican or a Democrat; it doesn't really matter here. But James was passionate about saying that Christianity is radically concerned with personal purity (don't be polluted by this world) and with practical, public compassion (care for the people no one else cares about). True Christianity is marked by both personal life and public life that demonstrate religion God our Father accepts as pure and faultless.

The second mark of true and acceptable religion is sacrificial care for those in need. We are to "look after" orphans and widows. That word literally means to "to seek out someone" or to "visit" them, and the implication is that you go to them in order to care for them. This is such a potent word in the New Testament. God uses it to describe how He visits His people to help them, to strengthen them, to encourage them (Luke 1:68,78; 7:16; Acts 15:14).[3] When James wrote this letter,

---

[3] For definitions and uses of the word *episkeptomai*, see BDAG, 378.

there was no life insurance a husband or father would leave to a widow or his children, nor were there government-run programs to provide for them. As the Old Testament story of Ruth shows us, widows and orphans were desolate and destitute. James tells us that true religion consists in looking after the neediest people in your community. He's not just saying that if you are a Christian, this is one way you might help someone else. No, he's saying that if you are a Christian, you are obligated to look after orphans and widows, and if you don't, your religion is not acceptable before God.

We are to help orphans and widows because **they are helpless**. For the widow or the widower, the deceased spouse creates a void. God is the defender, sustainer, strength, and provider for such people, and His provision comes through the hearts and lives of His people.

Moreover, millions of children lack a parent to wake them up, to play with them, to read to them, and to tuck them in at night. And they are not just on the other side of the world; they are in our community right around us as well. There are 400,000 children in the U.S. foster care system, over 100,000 of whom are waiting for and wanting a parent to adopt them (AFCARS). James is saying what God says throughout Scripture: **we must be selfless**, we must not neglect them. Remember, this is religion God *our Father* accepts. He is Father to the fatherless, and He shows it through His people. Looking after orphans and widows is not an option for the church; it is an obligation for the church.

Clear Separation from the Ways of the World (1:27–2:13)

Many people think James is simply speaking of being morally pure, but I'm convinced there's a key link here between the end of James 1:27 and the beginning of James 2. James mentions the "world" three other times in this letter (2:5; 3:6; 4:4), and each time he is referring to the fallen world system that runs contrary to the ways of God. The implication here at the end of James 1:27 is that we are supposed to be holy, but James defines *holiness* as going against the grain of the world, not living according to the system of this world. James immediately applies this truth in 1:27 to the issue of favoritism in chapter 2.

Favoritism is a common way the church (then and now) slides into worldliness. The world loves to honor the rich and neglect the poor, and James is saying that the church, if it's not careful, will honor the rich and neglect the poor as well. He says not to show favoritism in 2:1, for faith and favoritism are completely incompatible. He begins this illustration by talking about how the church was favoring the rich above the poor, the very thing the world does. In the world's system you honor, respect, and treat well the person who can benefit you the most. Is that what we're doing as followers of Christ today?

At this point we could consider churches we've been a part of where leadership was determined by how much money someone made. If someone had a lot of money, they had a lot of influence in the church. This is sad, and there is no room for it in the church. But have we stopped to consider why we spend what we do on nice buildings and elaborate programs? Is it to appeal to the poor? No, we have designed our buildings and created our programs (maybe unknowingly, but ultimately) to appeal to the rich. People who are rich expect excellence, nice things, and comfort. They expect to feel good, and we have spent God's resources trying to appeal to them. We have not had the poor on our minds at all. It's almost as if we have said to the poor, "Sit at our feet and we will throw you our scraps." We are guilty of favoritism, and in this way we are virtually indistinguishable from the system of the world. We need to repent. But how?

Showing favoritism is ingrained in us. It's so natural for us to want to attract those who will most benefit us. This is where we see five glorious reminders James gave the church in his day that we must remember as the church in our day.

We are captivated by the glory of Christ. James says in 2:1, "My brothers, do not show favoritism as you hold on to the faith in our glorious Lord Jesus Christ." This is only the second time James refers to Jesus directly in this letter (though the teachings of Christ are throughout this book).[4] There are some slight differences in how to translate the phrase "glorious Lord Jesus Christ,"[5] but the emphasis here is on the glory of God being embodied in the person of Christ, that is, Christ's splendor, majesty, and supremacy over and above all. If we are captivated by this, then we will not show favoritism for at least two reasons.

We will not show favoritism when **we see Christ's supremacy over the wealthy**. The church in James was giving honor where honor was not due. You don't honor the wealthy because they are rich in money; you honor Christ because He is rich in glory. Only Christ is supreme,

---

[4] The only other direct reference to Jesus in this letter occurs in the opening verse, where James refers to himself as a "servant of God and of the Lord Jesus Christ."

[5] The ESV has "Lord Jesus Christ, the Lord of glory."

so we focus our eyes on Him. We will also put aside favoritism when **we remember His sacrifice for the needy**. Jesus Christ, the Lord of glory, came down to the lowly and despised, sinners like you and me; and He gave His life for the poorest of the poor in order that we might be rich in him. Second Corinthians 8:9 says it like this: "For you know the grace of our Lord Jesus Christ: Though He was rich, for your sake He became poor, so that by His poverty you might become rich." You can't show favoritism when you know this Christ, when you are captivated by the Lord of glory who gave His everything so that you might be rich in Him. You don't attribute too much to the wealthy, and the last thing you do is look down on the poor because this is exactly who Christ came for—*you* in all your poverty. See how the gospel transforms the way we live!

We are gripped by the grace of Christ. After he finishes the illustration about the rich and the poor entering the church's meeting in verses 1-4, James says that God chose the poor to be "rich in faith" (v. 5). God, by His grace, throughout redemptive history has delighted in showing His grace to the poor of this world. This truth abounds in every part of the Old and New Testaments. Consider just two representative examples regarding the physically poor:

> *God, You provided for the poor by Your goodness.* (Ps 68:10)

> *They asked only that we would remember the poor, which I made every effort to do.* (Gal 2:10)

These words concerning the physical poor are accompanied throughout Scripture by mention of the spiritually poor. Take for example this famous quote from the Sermon on the Mount:

> *The poor in spirit are blessed, for the kingdom of heaven is theirs.*
> (Matt 5:3)

This is the testimony of Scripture: God has chosen to show His grace greatly to the poor—to those who suffer with physical needs, and most importantly to those who acknowledge their spiritual need. So similarly here, James says that by neglecting the poor we are negating the grace that lies at the heart of God.

And this is where we remember that **Christ reverses our status in this world**. This is a summary of much of Jesus' ministry in the Gospels: "He has satisfied the hungry with good things and sent the rich away empty" (Luke 1:53). This is also the story of Paul's letters:

*Brothers, consider your calling: Not many are wise from a human
perspective, not many powerful, not many of noble birth. Instead, God
has chosen what is foolish in the world to shame the wise, and God has
chosen what is weak in the world to shame the strong. God has chosen
what is insignificant and despised in the world—what is viewed as
nothing—to bring to nothing what is viewed as something, so that no
one can boast in His presence.* (1 Cor 1:26-29)

Those who are poor in spirit and neglected in this world can find in
Christ a richness of spirit that leads to glory in the world to come.

Not only does Christ reverse our status in this world, but also **Christ
transforms our standards in this world**. James is asking, "Do you realize
whom you are honoring?" These believers were honoring those who
were oppressing and taking advantage of God's people. They wanted
the favor of those who were far from God. Now, I want to be careful
not to imply that poverty is equated with righteousness and wealth with
wickedness. We're not sure about the exact cultural situation James is
addressing, but the point is clear. When we look at a man, we look at
the outward appearance—the car he drives, the clothes he wears, the
house he lives in, the lifestyle he leads—and we often honor him based
on these things. But Scripture turns all of that upside down and tells us
to look at men through the lens of the grace of God in Christ. This is
key in terms of how we view and treat others. We ought to see everyone
through the eyes of Christ. We ought to look at brothers and sisters
around us, regardless of wealth or socioeconomic status, as those who,
like us, are united to Christ, for Christ lives in them. We also need to
see men and women around us who are not Christians as those whom
Christ created, as those whom He loves, as those He desires to know
Him. Let's put aside the standards of this world and see one another
through the eyes of the Word, in relation to Christ.

We are devoted to the law of Christ. In verse 8, James starts speaking
about "the royal law prescribed in the Scripture." James is quoting
here from Leviticus 19:18 when God says to love your neighbor as yourself. And when he speaks about the law, he's not talking about all the
Levitical laws, moral codes, and dietary laws. He's talking about the law
understood as the commands of God ultimately fulfilled in Christ and
understood in light of Christ. This law is summed up in the two great
commandments: love God with all your heart, soul, mind, and strength,
and love your neighbor as yourself (see Mark 12:28-31; Deut 6:4). The
context of this command in Leviticus 19 gives us a pretty strong sense

of what James is getting at when he cites this Old Testament passage. Verses 15-18 read as follows:

You must not act unjustly when deciding a case. Do not be partial to the poor or give preference to the rich; judge your neighbor fairly. You must not go about spreading slander among your people; you must not jeopardize your neighbor's life; I am Yahweh.

You must not harbor hatred against your brother. Rebuke your neighbor directly, and you will not incur guilt because of him. Do not take revenge or bear a grudge against members of your community, but love your neighbor as yourself; I am Yahweh.

God said in Leviticus 19 to be just and not to show favoritism but instead to love your neighbor as yourself. Likewise Jesus said in the Gospels to love your neighbor as yourself (see Matt 22:39; Mark 12:31).

Then James comes on the scene and says that if you keep this royal law, you are doing right, but if you show favoritism and thus disobey this law, then you are a lawbreaker. James is bringing home the reality that to show favoritism is sin. It is a violation of the law of love, the law of Christ; and when you show favoritism, you are guilty of breaking the law on two fronts.

First, **favoritism disrespects man.** The word *favoritism* in the original language of the NT literally means to "receive according to the face," or in other words, to make judgments about people based on external appearance (Moo, *James*, 102).[6] To make such judgments is not in any way to love your neighbor as yourself. James deals with this issue in terms of rich and poor, and appropriately so in light of the context of this passage, but we show favoritism in other ways. Favoritism is present any time we are making judgments about people based on external appearance. This could be according to dress, general physical appearance, color of skin, or a host of other characteristics. As the people of God, we must be on guard against this sin because it is often subtle and almost unnoticed.

Favoritism often shows up, for example, on the basis of ethnicity.[7] Imagine walking into a lunchroom by yourself, and you see two tables.

---

[6] Moo notes that the word here is plural so that it has "wide-ranging application" (*James*, 102).

[7] I'm deliberately not using the term *race* here because of a theological understanding that we are all of the same race, the race of Adam, which is key to understanding our unity in Christ.

One table has a group of people ethnically like you, and the other table has a group of people ethnically not like you. What do you instinctively do? You gravitate toward the people who are like you. But why? What is the mental impulse that leads us to make that decision? I don't want to oversimplify this, but it goes something like this, at the speed of thought: *One group is not like me, and one group is like me. The group like me is safer, and therefore more comfortable, and more comfortable means there is more to gain.* At the speed of thought, you are drawn instinctively toward those who are like you. The opposite thought process goes on when we think of the other table that is not like us. *They are not like me and therefore not safe, which means they are not comfortable, and thus I have nothing to gain.* James says not to think like this. Don't respond to one another according to the face, according to the outer appearance.

I'm guessing in our day we would embrace the idea that we should not show favoritism, but we have a long way to go in living out this reality. Consider how we talk: People say, "I met a Korean guy the other day," or "I was talking with a Hispanic guy." Why does it matter that he was Korean or Hispanic? Do you usually say, "I met a white guy the other day?" or "I was talking with a black guy?" Why do we feel the need to point out how people are different from us unnecessarily?

Favoritism disrespects man, and ultimately **favoritism dishonors God Himself**. James tells us that when you break one law, you are guilty of breaking all the law (2:10), and in the process you offend the One who gives the law. To show favoritism toward man is to dishonor God. This is a serious charge, which is what leads James to the next reminder.

We are cognizant of the judgment of Christ. In 2:12-13 James says, "Speak and act as those who will be judged by the law of freedom. For judgment is without mercy to the one who hasn't shown mercy." Because favoritism is such a serious sin, James immediately takes us to an awareness of divine judgment and reminds us that we will be judged according to our consistency of speech and action.

In short, **our words will be judged**. In Matthew 12:36-37 Jesus says,

> I tell you that on the day of judgment people will have to account for every careless word they speak. For by your words you will be acquitted, and by your words you will be condemned.

That will make you think twice before texting, posting something on social media, or speaking.

While words are a reflection of our heart, we shouldn't miss how our works relate to judgment, both for Jesus and for James. According to Scripture, **our deeds (or lack thereof) will be judged**. You might think, "This doesn't make sense in the New Testament—someone like Paul would never speak like this." However, consider what the apostle Paul says in Romans 2:6-11:

> *He will repay each one according to his works: eternal life to those who by persistence in doing good seek glory, honor, and immortality; but wrath and indignation to those who are self-seeking and disobey the truth but are obeying unrighteousness; affliction and distress for every human being who does evil, first to the Jew, and also to the Greek; but glory, honor, and peace for everyone who does what is good, first to the Jew, and also to the Greek. There is no favoritism with God.*

We find a similar idea in 2 Corinthians 5:10, where Paul says, "For we must all appear before the tribunal of Christ, so that each may be repaid for what he has done in the body, whether good or worthless." Like Paul, James is telling us not to play around with favoritism, with our words, or with our actions. We will be judged for how we respond to what God has said is important.

Remember what Jesus Himself said when he was speaking to those who didn't feed the hungry, clothe the naked, or help the poor: "Depart from Me, you who are cursed, into the eternal fire prepared for the Devil and his angels!" (Matt 25:41). You will stand before God to give an account for your words, your actions, or your lack of action when it comes to that which God has said is most important—to love your neighbor as yourself. So speak with love and act with love.

Now you might be thinking, "How can I speak and act well enough to be OK before God? I could never do that." And this is where you recognize that you could never do enough to stand before the judgment seat of Christ, and so you subsequently realize that you need Christ's mercy. That leads to our last reminder from James on this point.

We are a reflection of the mercy of Christ. The message of the gospel is that we all need mercy. We need mercy that "triumphs over judgment" (2:13). Praise God that He brings justice and mercy together in the cross, and you and I can be declared right before God based on the righteousness of Jesus Christ. James is saying that when you have experienced that kind of mercy, you clearly know how to show mercy to others. God's mercy *in* you overflows *from* you.

As we have received mercy, so we extend mercy. Just as Jesus taught in the Sermon on the Mount, "For if you forgive people their wrongdoing, your heavenly Father will forgive your as well. But if you don't forgive people, your Father will not forgive your wrongdoing" (Matt 6:14-15). When you are forgiven of your sins, you are compelled to forgive others. As you have received mercy, you extend mercy. But the converse of this truth is particularly humbling and penetrating: **if we do not extend mercy, we demonstrate that we have not received mercy.** James says that judgment without mercy will be shown to anyone who has not been merciful (2:13). This is not saying we need to be merciful to others in order to earn mercy before God. You can't earn mercy; it's mercy because it can't be earned. No, this text is saying you can tell who has received mercy from God by the way they show mercy to others. If mercy is evident in someone's life, then clearly Christ by His mercy is dwelling in them. But if mercy is not evident in them, then there may be reason to wonder whether Christ by His mercy is dwelling in them.

The Manifestation of True and Acceptable Religion

This discussion of showing mercy brings us back to the idea we began with, namely that authentic religion, or faith, must be evident in our actions. If we do not keep a tight rein on our tongue, then our religion is worthless (1:26). If our words and works do not reflect the mercy of God, then we show that we do not have faith in Christ (2:12-13). Religion that God accepts as pure and faultless is to look after orphans and widows and to keep oneself from being polluted by the world (1:27). If we fail to do these things, then we show that we have not really been transformed by the life-giving mercy of Christ, and our religion is not acceptable before God. Christ produces mercy in His people, which changes the way they act and speak before others. That's the point of this text, for **faith always expresses itself through love**.

Reflect and Discuss

1. Name some specific ways in which our Christian culture has twisted the message of New Testament Christianity.
2. Why is the term *religion* viewed so negatively among some Christians? How does James use the word?
3. How can you set an example for other followers of Christ by your speech and conversation? What habits of speech do you need to repent of?
4. What's the danger of separating personal holiness from compassion for those in need? Which one of these do you find yourself ignoring?
5. What has your attitude been toward orphans and widows? What are some practical steps you could take to begin to care for those around you?
6. What are some ways you have shown favoritism, maybe even unintentionally, to those in your circle of influence? How have you seen favoritism play out in your church?
7. How should Christ's judgment on the last day affect your words and actions today? Does this contradict God's grace? Explain your answer.
8. Why does showing mercy depend on receiving mercy, and how does the message of the gospel fit into this?
9. How does care for the poor in our communities and around the world affect our gospel witness?
10. List some ways in which James's teaching mirrors the ministry and teaching of Jesus in the Gospels.

Faith Acts

JAMES 2:14-19

Main Idea: Faith in our hearts is evident in the fruit of our lives.

I. **Three Main Truths**
   A. Faith in our hearts is evident in the fruit of our lives (2:14).
   B. People who fail to help poverty-stricken fellow believers are in fact not saved (2:15-17).
      1. Acts of mercy are not means to salvation.
      2. Acts of mercy are necessary evidence of salvation.
   C. Ultimately, deedless faith is useless faith (2:18).
II. **Three Key Conclusions (2:19)**
   A. Faith is not mere intellectual assent.
   B. Faith is not simply an emotional response.
   C. Faith involves willful obedience.

In this passage James converses with an imaginary person, a person who claims to have faith but has no deeds, a person who claims that you can separate faith from works. This was obviously a common thought among James's readers, so he addresses it squarely and strongly. We need to walk through these verses carefully and patiently because the possibilities for misunderstanding here abound. We need to see clearly and accurately what Scripture is saying, and along the way we need to consider how these verses fit with the entirety of Scripture's teaching on faith and works and how these verses radically challenge and change our lives.

Three Main Truths

There are three main truths in this passage, and in a sense each repeats this same basic reality: faith without works is dead (vv. 17,20,26). Now, what does it mean for faith to be dead? It means it doesn't save (v. 14), it doesn't justify us before God (v. 24). It is not alive. It is dead, which means it doesn't really exist.

The noun *faith* appears 16 times in the book of James, 11 of which are in this passage (Stein, "Saved by Faith," 4–19). In the five times the word *faith* is found outside of this passage, it is always used positively: 1:3,6; 2:1,5; 5:15. But of the 11 times it is used in this passage, eight are used in connection with this imaginary person who claims to have faith but has no deeds. The point of the passage is that this person doesn't really have faith. He claims to have it, but he doesn't. His so-called faith is dead and worthless. It does not save; quite literally, it does not work.[8] Understanding this is important because James is not contrasting someone who has immature faith with someone who has mature faith, or someone who has nominal faith with someone who has authentic faith. He's telling us that you either have faith that saves or you don't—there's no in-between.

Faith in Our Hearts Is Evident in the Fruit of Our Lives (2:14)

From the beginning in 2:14, James is saying it's possible to claim to have faith but not actually have it—to claim to have faith but not be saved. So how do you know if someone has faith that saves? James tells us to look for fruit. Now, he's not saying we need to add deeds to faith in order to be saved. He is saying that deeds are the fruit of faith, and that real, true, genuine faith produces fruit. This means that if there is no fruit, then clearly there is no faith. This is the same thing Jesus said in the Sermon on the Mount:

> *You'll recognize them by their fruit. Are grapes gathered from thornbushes or figs from thistles? In the same way, every good tree produces good fruit, but a bad tree produces bad fruit. A good tree can't produce bad fruit; neither can a bad tree produce good fruit. Every tree that doesn't produce good fruit is cut down and thrown into the fire. So you'll recognize them by their fruit.* (Matt 7:16-20)

If you look at a tree with apples hanging from its limbs, you know it's an apple tree. What is on the outside is evidence of what is on the inside. That's what James is saying. Fruit in our lives is evidence of faith in our hearts. And if there is no fruit, there is no faith. It's that simple. You will know faith by its fruit. This simple truth sets the stage for a jaw-dropping truth in verses 15-17 that is illustrated by a hypothetical situation.

---

[8] Blomberg and Kamell point out the pun James uses here, as faith without works is referred to as "workless" (*James*, 136).

People Who Fail to Help Poverty-Stricken Fellow Believers Are in Fact Not Saved (2:15-17)

This may sound harsh to some people, but is this not the clear truth of James 2:15-17? James mentions a brother or sister who is "without clothes and lacks daily food" (v. 15). In their poverty they don't even have covering from the cold as they stand shamed and miserable. They literally don't have "food for the day"; they're starving because they are unable to sustain themselves. This is not mild need; this is dire, desperate need. And then you say to that person, "Go in peace, keep warm, and eat well" (v. 16). The language is a common benediction, even a prayer that you would say over someone: "Go in peace," or "I pray you have a great day." It's shocking to think of saying to such a person, "Keep warm and well fed." The verbs in this latter phrase are either in the middle or passive voice, which means they could be translated one of two ways: Either the person is saying, "Warm and feed yourself" (middle voice), as if he could, or "Stay warmed and well fed" (passive voice), which almost suggests that he already has all he needs.[9] James asks of that kind of faith, "What good is it?" (v. 16). In the same way, faith like that does not help that other person in need; faith like that does not save your own soul (Blomberg and Kamell, *James*, 131).[10] That kind of faith is dead. It's not faith at all.

People who claim to be Christians but fail to help poverty-stricken fellow believers are in fact not saved. Their faith is dead. Now you can do cartwheels all around this text to try to find your way out of this truth, but it is there. Someone who responds like this to a brother or sister without clothes and daily food does not have faith that saves. This is exactly what 1 John 3:17 says: "If anyone has this world's goods and sees his brother in need but closes his eyes to his need—how can God's love reside in him?" The implication is that it can't.

---

[9] Blomberg and Kamell note that the use of the passive here—"be warmed and filled"—leaves us with the question, "How did the person in a position to help think the poor person would receive aid?" (*James*, 131). The works of Laws and Johnson are cited on this point (131): Laws refers to this phrase as a way of saying that one hoped God would supply the need, which according to Johnson makes this "reprehensible" as a "religious cover for the failure to act." Sophie Laws, *The Epistle of James*, 121. Luke T. Johnson, *The Letter of James*, 239.

[10] For more on the inadequacy of a faith that doesn't meet the essential needs of fellow believers, see the discussion on 130–32.

Now two reminders are extremely important as we consider this second point made by James. First, **acts of mercy are not means to salvation**. We are not saved by what we do. James is not teaching that we are saved by our actions. He has already showed us this in 1:17-18,21; 2:5. James has made clear that faith is something God gives, not something we manufacture. This cannot be emphasized enough: We are saved by the abundant grace and glorious initiative of God. Acts of mercy are not means to salvation. We don't help the poor in order to be saved. Rather than being the *means* to salvation, **acts of mercy are necessary evidence of salvation**. We might also call acts of mercy the natural overflow of salvation.

James never speaks of deeds we do in order to earn favor before God. That would be a works-righteousness approach to deeds. Instead, James always speaks of deeds as fruit produced by faith in Christ. This is simply a reiteration of the last truth, that the fruit of faith is mercy toward the poor. And if there is no mercy toward the poor, there is no faith. Tim Keller, the pastor of Redeemer Church in New York City, a church reaching out in mercy ministry across that city and around the world, said: "Mercy to the full range of human needs is such an essential mark of a Christian that it can be used as a test of true faith. Mercy is not optional or an addition to being a Christian. Rather, a life poured out in deeds of mercy is the sign of genuine faith" (*Ministries of Mercy*, 35).

Keller's point and the point James has been making in this passage is crystal clear in Matthew 25:31-34:

> *When the Son of Man comes in His glory, and all the angels with Him, then He will sit on the throne of His glory. All the nations will be gathered before Him, and He will separate them one from another, just as a shepherd separates the sheep from the goats. He will put the sheep on His right and the goats on the left. Then the King will say to those on His right, "Come, you who are blessed by My Father, inherit the kingdom prepared for you from the foundation of the world."*

Did you catch that language? Jesus speaks of those who are "blessed by My Father" as those who will "inherit the kingdom prepared for you from the foundation of the world." Do you feel the grace in these verses? God has blessed these people, and He has given them the kingdom prepared since the creation of the world. This is the mercy of God. But see how the mercy of God transforms what they do. Consider the first person pronouns in verses 35-36 and remember that this is Jesus talking:

> *For* I *was hungry and you gave* Me *something to eat;*
> I *was thirsty and you gave* Me *something to drink;*
> I *was a stranger and you took* Me *in;*
> I *was naked and you clothed* Me*;*
> I *was sick and you took care of*[11] Me*;*
> I *was in prison and you visited* Me. (emphasis added)

Then listen to the response of the righteous in verses 37-40:

> *Then the righteous will answer Him, "Lord, when did we see You
> hungry and feed You, or thirsty and give You something to drink?
> When did we see You a stranger and take You in, or without clothes
> and clothe You? When did we see You sick, or in prison, and visit
> You?"*
>
> *And the King will answer them, "I assure you: Whatever you did
> for one of the least of these brothers of Mine, you did for Me."*

Ministering to a poor brother or sister in Christ is equated with ministering to Christ Himself. In a real way Christ is in that brother or sister to whom you are ministering in their need. So is it possible for a Christian to see Christ hungry and not feed Him? Is it possible for a Christian to see Christ thirsty and not give Him something to drink? Absolutely not. The overflow of the Christian's heart is to serve, and the Christian's external acts of mercy are clear evidence of the internal mercy of God in his heart.

Now see the other side of the picture in Matthew 25:41-46:

> *Then He will also say to those on the left, "Depart from Me, you who
> are cursed, into the eternal fire prepared for the Devil and his angels!*
> *For I was hungry and you gave Me nothing to eat;*
> *I was thirsty and you gave Me nothing to drink;*
> *I was a stranger and you didn't take Me in;*
> *I was naked and you didn't clothe Me,*
> *sick and in prison and you didn't take care of Me."*
> *Then they too will answer, "Lord, when did we see You hungry, or
> thirsty, or a stranger, or without clothes, or sick, or in prison, and not
> help You?"*

---

[11] The same word—*episkeptomai*—translated here as "took care of" is used in James 1:27 to speak of looking after orphans and widows.

> *Then He will answer them, "I assure you: Whatever you did not
> do for one of the least of these, you did not do for Me either."*
> *And they will go away into eternal punishment, but the righteous
> into eternal life.*

Those who do not feed the hungry or clothe the poor depart into eternal fire because their hearts have clearly not been transformed by mercy. These people lack faith in Christ, which their lack of mercy clearly demonstrates. Again, acts of mercy are not the means of salvation; they are the necessary evidence.

This point is so important because we must remember that guilt is not the motivation for caring for the poor. We don't provide for the poor because we must. No, the gospel motivates us to care for the poor. We provide for the poor because we are compelled by the mercy of God that has radically transformed our hearts, and His mercy overflows from our lives. I love what Charles Spurgeon said about why the saints fed the hungry and clothed the naked in Matthew 25:

> The saints fed the hungry and clothed the naked because it
> gave them much pleasure to do so. They did it because they
> could not help doing it, their new nature impelled them to it.
> They did it because it was their delight to do good. . . . They
> did good for Christ's sake, because it was the sweetest thing
> in the world to do anything for Jesus. (Spurgeon, "The Final
> Separation," 288)

This is faith, and if this fruit (the fruit of providing for the poor) is not evident in our lives, then it is clear that we do not have faith. People who claim to be Christians but fail to help poverty-stricken fellow believers are in fact not saved.

Ultimately, Deedless Faith Is Useless Faith (2:18)

All of this leads to the third and final truth in this passage, which is in a sense a reiteration of all that we have seen so far. James continues this dialogue and imagines someone separating faith and deeds. For example, some people are merciful toward the poor; others aren't. People are just different. This imaginary "someone" James is talking about is trying to separate faith from deeds, and James says, "You can't do it." Works, deeds, and actions are not optional for those who have faith; they are inevitable. Your faith is nonexistent if there are no deeds.

In verse 20, James reiterates the point he has just shown us: "Foolish man! Are you willing to learn that faith without works is useless?" Faith without works is useless to your brother and sister who still have no clothes and no food. It is also useless to you because it cannot save you.

Three Key Conclusions
JAMES 2:19

James makes three things about faith abundantly clear. First, **faith is not mere intellectual assent**. In verse 19 he says, "You believe that God is one; you do well. The demons also believe—and they shudder." Every Jewish man or woman believed the Shema[12] in Deuteronomy 6:4: "Listen, Israel: The LORD our God, the LORD is One." The demons believe the Shema. Demons believe a lot of things that we believe—they believe in the existence of God, the deity of Christ, and the presence of heaven and hell. They know Christ is the eternal Judge, and they know that Christ alone is able to save. I fear that countless men and women have bought into the soul-damning idea that mere intellectual assent to the truth of God in Christ is enough to save, and the reality is that these people are no better off than the demons themselves.

Second, **faith is not simply an emotional response**. According to James 2:19, the faith of demons is not just intellectual but also emotional. The demons believe and they "shudder." They are affected by the truth of God; they tremble at it. I wonder how many people define their faith today merely by the emotions they feel at any given time.

The third point James makes about faith is that **faith involves willful obedience**. You show your faith not just by what you think or by what you feel but by what you do. Faith acts. If your faith consists merely of listening to the Word, talking about the Word, or feeling a certain way about the Word, your faith is dead. Faith acts on the Word. Faith in our hearts is evident in the fruit of our lives.

---

[12] The word *shema* is a transliteration of a Hebrew verb that means to hear or listen. It is the first word in the Hebrew of Deuteronomy 6:4.

Reflect and Discuss

1. Respond to this statement: It is unloving to question whether someone has genuine biblical faith.
2. How would you define biblical faith to an unbeliever?
3. If not even mature Christians are sinless, how can we hope to meet James's standard in this passage?
4. What does your treatment of those in need reveal about your faith?
5. Given that we have limited time and resources, what is our responsibility to the needy?
6. Why is it so easy to blur the line between doing a good work as a means to salvation and doing a good work as evidence of salvation?
7. What counsel would you give to a friend who believes the teachings of Scripture but has no spiritual fruit?
8. What counsel would you give to another believer who has evidence of genuine faith but who never feels like he or she measures up to God's standard?
9. How is mere intellectual assent similar to demonic faith?
10. If God ultimately produces spiritual fruit in our lives, what role do we play in pursuing greater maturity in the faith?

Faith Sacrifices

JAMES 2:20-24

Main Idea: The faith that saves always produces good works and is based on God's saving work in Jesus Christ.

I. **Two Pictures of Faith (2:20)**
    A. Dead faith, which does not save
    B. Living faith, which does save
II. **Two Pictures of Righteousness (2:21)**
    A. Positional righteousness: how we stand before God
    B. Practical righteousness: how we live before God
III. **Two Pictures of Works (2:22-24)**
    A. Works fueled by the flesh, which do not honor God
    B. Works that are the fruit of faith, which bring great glory to God
IV. **Two Pictures of Justification (2:24)**
    A. Initial justification
    B. Final justification
V. **Two Truths to Remember**
    A. Salvation is through faith
    B. Faith works

James 2:20-24 is one of the most difficult passages about salvation in all of the New Testament. This difficulty becomes evident when we put two passages of Scripture side by side: James 2:24 and Romans 3:28.

You see that a man is justified by works and not by faith alone. (Jas 2:24)

For we conclude that a man is justified by faith apart from the works of the law. (Rom 3:28)

In James 2:24 we read that a person is justified by what he does, not by faith alone. Then in Romans 3:28 we read that a man is justified by faith apart from works. So, which is it?

It is helpful to keep the whole context of 2:14-24 in mind. In a sense James 2:24 summarizes the whole book of James. Likewise, in a sense Romans 3:28 summarizes the whole book of Romans. So, what are we to do? How are we to understand this? The contrast between these two passages is one of the reasons Martin Luther once called James an "epistle of straw" ("Preface," 362) and that he almost felt like "throwing Jimmy into the stove" ("Licentiate," 317). However, we have no reason to shrink back from either James or Paul because they do not contradict one another. Each of them is writing about the exact same gospel; yet they are writing from different vantage points, and they are addressing different problems in the churches to whom they are writing. I don't picture James and Paul standing toe-to-toe with each other with contrary understandings of the gospel. Instead, they are standing back-to-back with each other fighting two different enemies and together defending a unified understanding of the gospel. Paul is fighting against the false idea that we can earn our salvation with our works (which, by the way, is the same battle Luther was fighting in the Reformation when confronting the teachings of the Catholic Church). James, on the other hand, is fighting against an easy believism that had reduced salvation to intellectual belief. So, which battle are we fighting today? I think the answer is . . . both.

Many followers of Christ, whether they admit it or not, think they can work their way to God. As the shepherd of a local church, I want to fight against that idea with everything in me. At the same time, many others believe the idea that we are saved by grace through faith means works are irrelevant to God and obedience is unimportant. I also want to fight against that idea with everything in me.

This passage gives us a picture of a glorious gospel that is received by faith, but this faith is not mere intellectual belief. This is a faith that results in radical obedience to the commands of Christ, and we need to think more about what that kind of obedience looks like.

Some time ago I had the opportunity to preach in Germany. One day while I was there, some guys asked me if I would be interested in playing a pickup game of football with them. I used to play some flag football and loved doing that, so I told them, "Yes, I'm in." I walked with them down to the field only to discover not two goalposts and a brown ball but two goals with nets on them and a white-and-black checkered ball. That's when I realized that their understanding of football is a lot different from my understanding of football. I call their understanding of football "soccer"!

This is similar to the situation we have with James 2 and Romans 3. Understanding what James and Paul are saying is contingent on understanding how they are using certain words. You can have the same word with different meanings. This is true in all of life, and it's true in the Bible as well. In order to have effective communication, you need to understand what someone means when they use a certain word. As we walk through James 2, we need to stop at key words along the way in order to think about how those words are used in the Bible, oftentimes in different ways. In the process I want us to see that while the words James and Paul are using may initially seem contradictory, in the end these men are both clearly and boldly preaching the same gospel.

Interestingly, James uses Abraham as an example of what he is saying (2:21-23), and when you get over to Paul, guess who he uses as an example? Abraham (Rom 4:1-3)! Abraham is the model of faith for both of these biblical authors, and in Abraham's life, we're going to take the truths James and Paul teach and see them in action.

Two Pictures of Faith
JAMES 2:20

Here we read that faith without works is "useless." This is the point James made in 2:14-19, and it's vitally important for us to remember it, especially when we get to verse 24. Remember that in this passage James is not contrasting mature faith with immature faith or lukewarm faith with dynamic faith. No, he's contrasting genuine faith with professed faith that in fact doesn't exist. He is saying some people were claiming to have faith, but, for example, they don't care for the poor, and thus their so-called faith consists of nothing more than what demons have. James is saying this is not really faith. It's dead. It's nothing.

So in James we see two pictures of this word *faith*. First, we see **dead faith, which does not save**. As we've already seen in James, a person's faith that claims to believe in Jesus for salvation yet ignores the poor at his doorstep is not faith at all (2:14-17). James says this strongly in verse 20. He calls the man with no works a "foolish man!" The Greek word literally means "empty," and James is saying that the person is claiming to have faith without deeds, but the reality is that person has nothing. They don't have faith.

Second, contrasted with dead faith, James says there is a **living faith, which does save**. In every mention of faith in this epistle outside of this passage, James is talking about living faith: faith in our glorious Lord Jesus Christ (2:1) that perseveres through trial (1:3,6) and avoids favoritism (2:5). Yet in 2:14-24 James introduces imaginary people who claim to have faith without deeds, and James says over and over again that such people don't really have faith. And it's not only James who would not call this true faith; Paul wouldn't either. James and Paul would both say dead faith doesn't save.

So what about you: Is your faith dead or living? Is your faith only about intellectual assent to belief in God or Christ? Or is your faith alive, penetrating, and transforming every part of who you are? This is an eternally important question.

Two Pictures of Righteousness
JAMES 2:21

After seeing two different pictures of faith, we now turn to verse 21 to see two different pictures of righteousness. The word *righteousness* is used in various ways throughout Scripture, but two ways in particular are relevant to this passage. In fact, we see both of these understandings of righteousness within Paul's own writings. First, **positional righteousness** refers to **how we stand before God**. This is what happens at the initial point of our salvation. When you trust in Christ for salvation, by God's grace you are made right before God. Christ imputes, grants, and clothes you in His righteousness at the moment of your salvation (2 Cor 5:21), and you are made right before God. You, a sinner, have peace with God because of the righteousness of Jesus Christ.

But then Scripture also gives a picture of **practical righteousness**, which refers to **how we live before God**. We demonstrate and grow in righteousness in the way we live. These two understandings of righteousness are not totally separate and distinct from each other. Those who are counted as righteous in Christ practically manifest righteousness in their lives as they grow in the likeness of Christ.

So at times in Scripture, righteousness refers to how we stand before God, and at other times it refers to how we live before God. What James means here when he talks about "righteousness" is going to become clearer as we dive deeper into this passage.

Two Pictures of Works
JAMES 2:22-24

So far we've looked at two pictures of faith and two pictures of righteousness. Now we need to consider two pictures of works. James 2:22 says, "You see that faith was active together with his works, and by works, faith was perfected." The word *works* is sometimes translated "actions" and at other times "deeds." Most of the time these words go back to the same common Greek word *ergon*. When you see works/actions/deeds in the New Testament, you'll notice that Scripture sometimes refers to works in a positive way, and other times it refers to works in a negative way. Let's start with the negative.

Sometimes Scripture speaks of **works fueled by the flesh, which do not honor God**. This is the way Paul often talks about works. Paul talks about works of the law done in order to earn favor before God (Rom 3:28). Throughout Romans and Galatians Paul is speaking against people's attempt to attain salvation by their works. In Galatians people were being circumcised, obeying various laws, and abstaining from certain foods—all works done in an attempt to be righteous before God. But Paul says your works done to earn favor before God do not bring honor to God, and they do not save you. You cannot earn your way to God.

This is the danger of legalism, a danger we must always be on guard against. Legalism is believing that being right before God is ultimately a result of doing enough to earn His favor. That is decidedly what Paul is teaching against over and over again—works fueled by the flesh that do not honor God.

But legalism is not at all what James is talking about when he talks about works. James refers to works/deeds/actions 15 times, and every reference he uses is positive. Why? Because every time James talks about works, he is talking about **works that are the fruit of faith, which bring great glory to God**. When James talks about works, he is talking about God-glorifying obedience: love for the needy, mercy for the poor, care for the impoverished—all driven by the love and mercy of God. These things are the fruit of faith in God. Sometimes Paul talks about works in the same way. In Romans 1:5 he speaks of the "obedience of faith." First Thessalonians 1:3 and 2 Thessalonians 1:11 talk about the "work of faith." And in Galatians 5:6 Paul says, "What matters is faith working through love." So James and Paul are unified on this point. James is not advocating works in the flesh done to earn favor before God, and Paul rejoices in works produced by faith that bring glory to God. Both James and Paul see faith and works working together, which is exactly what James says in 2:20-24.

So with Abraham as our example, let's ask, "How does all of this work?" According to both James and Paul, **faith creates works**. James says in verses 22-23,

> *You see that faith was active together with his works, and by works, faith was perfected. So the Scripture was fulfilled that says, Abraham believed God, and it was credited to him for righteousness, and he was called God's friend.*

James quotes here from Genesis 15 and the story of Abraham. There's a progression in Abraham's life to which both Paul and James refer. God enters into covenant with Abraham, and here's how it happens:

> *After these events, the word of the LORD came to Abram in a vision:*
> *Do not be afraid, Abram.*
> *I am your shield;*
> *your reward will be very great.*
> *But Abram said, "Lord GOD, what can You give me, since I am childless and the heir of my house is Eliezer of Damascus?" Abram continued, "Look, You have given me no offspring, so a slave born in my house will be my heir."*
> *Now the word of the LORD came to him: "This one will not be your heir; instead, one who comes from your own body will be your heir." He took him outside and said, "Look at the sky and count the stars, if you are able to count them." Then He said to him, "Your offspring will be that numerous."*
> *Abram believed the LORD, and He credited it to him as righteousness.* (Gen 15:1-6)

God gave Abraham His promise, and Abraham believed God. Abraham's faith in God was credited to him as righteousness. Then we turn to Genesis 22 where God has given Abraham a son, Isaac. In verses 1-2 God tells Abraham to offer his son as a burnt offering. Abraham goes to the mountain with Isaac, raises the knife to sacrifice his only son, and then we read the following:

> *But the Angel of the LORD called to him from heaven and said,*
> *"Abraham, Abraham!"*
> *He replied, "Here I am."*

> *Then He said, "Do not lay a hand on the boy or do anything to him. For now I know that you fear God, since you have not withheld your only son from Me." (Gen 22:11-12)*

So when did Abraham first believe God? In Genesis 22? No. Abraham believed God a long time before that. Some scholars say that up to 30 years passed between Genesis 15 and 22. Abraham's faith resulted in works of obedience when God called him to sacrifice his son. And James is saying in chapter 2 that this is the fruit of faith. Just as when you take an apple seed and plant it in the ground, you will one day see an apple tree, so in the same way, when faith is born in a person's heart, it will bear fruit. By its nature faith creates works, and then in turn **works complete faith**. James says of Abraham in verse 22 that "by works, faith was perfected." Now, what does that word *perfected* mean? It means "to bring to maturity." Abraham's works matured his faith, brought his faith to its finished goal. James is saying that when we obey God (i.e., when we work), our faith grows up, matures, and is brought to completion.

To apply James's point practically, we might say the more you obey God, the more your faith grows. Faith leads you to obedience, and obedience matures faith. This is a wonderful reality. Works are good when they are the fruit of faith. Consider how this plays out in some of the most basic of Christian actions:

Coming to corporate worship. If you come to a worship gathering fueled by the flesh in order to put on a face before men or to earn favor before God, then this work of worship does not bring honor to God. But if your coming is the fruit of faith, if you believe and love God, and if you trust that He knows what He is saying when He tells us not to forsake gathering together (Heb 10:25), your actions do honor God. When your faith drives you to corporate worship with God's people, leading you to sing spiritual songs, listen to the Word of God, and fellowship with other believers, this is a part of bringing your faith to maturity.

Spending concentrated time in prayer and Bible study. If you are doing these things in the flesh because you feel like this is a religious routine you must do in order to earn favor before God, then this is not a good work. But if you believe your supreme delight is found in God and you want to know Him, hear from Him, and express the longings of your heart to Him, then a quiet time is a really good work.

Caring for the poor. If you do this in the flesh because you feel like you have to in order to earn favor before God, then caring for the poor will not bring honor to God. But if you believe God when He says this is important to Him and His people are to spend themselves on behalf of the poor, then you will care radically for the poor, and your faith will be made complete in what you do.

I love what Luther said about faith: "O it is a living, busy, active, mighty thing, this faith. It is impossible for it not to be doing good works incessantly. It does not ask whether good works are to be done, but before the question is asked, it has already done them, and is constantly doing them" ("Preface," 370).

We now move to verse 24, the most controversial verse in this passage: "You see that a man is justified by works and not by faith alone." So what does James mean that we are not justified by "faith alone"? We have to remember that throughout this passage James is talking with imaginary people who claim to have faith but don't really have it. Such faith is dead; it's not really faith at all. Thus, when we get to verse 24, James is communicating the same thing. He's saying, once again, that this kind of faith does not justify. It does not save. Why? Because this so-called faith is not really faith at all. All James is saying is that we are not justified by faith that claims to believe in Jesus but does nothing. This kind of faith is no different from demons' belief, and ultimately it is dead. And to that Paul himself would say, "Amen." When James refers to "faith alone" in verse 24, he is not talking about the same kind of faith Paul talks about or even the same kind of faith he (James) himself talks about in the rest of the book of James, namely, living faith. No, when James says "faith alone" in verse 24, he is referring to the dead, demonic, intellectual faith that he is countering throughout this passage.

Two Pictures of Justification
JAMES 2:24

We've seen there is no contradiction between James and Paul on the fact that living faith produces works, but there is still another big idea at the beginning of verse 24 that needs to be examined. James says a man is justified "by works." In other words, works, in some sense, play into our justification. This leads us to the last word we need to think about: justification.

A simple definition of justification is "to be declared right." As we think about salvation, the picture is that we are declared right before God. But how are we declared right before God? By faith or by works?

The answer to this question is huge, and the gospel hinges on it. This is where Paul and James both use Abraham to talk about justification, but interestingly they reference different points in Abraham's life. Paul's main point in the book of Romans is that Abraham was justified by faith before he did anything. Before he was circumcised, before he had Isaac, before he was willing to sacrifice Isaac, before all of this, Abraham had faith, and his faith was credited as righteousness (Rom 4:3). But James is emphasizing something altogether different. He is talking about when Abraham was willing to sacrifice Isaac in obedience to God, and James says that Abraham was considered righteous when he did that. In these two perspectives on Abraham's life—one from the standpoint of his initial faith and the other looking back on his life of obedience—separated by some 30 years, we see two pictures of justification.

First, when Paul talks about justification, he is most often talking about **initial justification**, which is **the inception of the Christian's life**. When you turn from yourself and trust in Jesus as the only One who can save you, God clothes you with the righteousness of Christ and by His grace declares you right before Him (Rom 4:3-5; Gal 2:16). In Ephesians 2:8 Paul says, "For you are saved by grace through faith, and this is not from yourselves; it is God's gift." See the danger Paul wants us to **avoid: thinking that works are a necessary basis or means of our salvation**. Paul in Scripture is calling us to believe in God, not in the sense that demons believe (which James is combating in 2:19), but in the sense that you believe Jesus is the sovereign Lord and King who alone has paid the price for your sins on the cross and who has finished the work of salvation for you so that nothing more is to be added to that work. Believe in Him and be saved. That's what Paul means when he talks about justification in Romans 3:21-26: at the moment you trust in Christ, you are justified before God. But that doesn't mean James is using the word in the same way.

In the Old Testament and in Jesus' teachings, this term *justification* is oftentimes used in reference not just to the initial point of salvation but to the final judgment where we will stand before God.

In Matthew 12:37 Jesus says, "For by your words you will be acquitted, and by your words you will be condemned." The word there for "acquitted" is akin to being "justified." Jesus is saying that by your words you will be declared innocent, and the picture here is of something that will happen in the future at the day of judgment. When we come to

James, who has already shown us how much he leans on Jesus' teachings and who has already talked about the judgment of God that is coming (2:12-13), it seems clear that he is not referring to initial justification, that is, the time when we first believe and are declared right before God but rather to **final justification**. Final justification refers to what will happen on the day of judgment when God declares us right in His sight. As opposed to talking about the inception of the Christian's life, James is talking about **the confirmation of the Christian's life**. This is what happens on the final day when what was declared initially is declared openly.

What James is confronting in his letter is different from what Paul is confronting. Paul wants us to avoid thinking we need to work in order to earn salvation. Then there's the danger James wants us to **avoid: thinking that works are not necessary as evidence of our salvation**. Again, works are not the basis of our justification. Final justification is not based on our works, but rather James is wanting us to see that when we stand before God on the day of judgment, it will be clear whether we had real, true, and authentic faith or dead, demonic faith.

You may ask, "How will I know if my faith was real?" And the answer is, "Was there any fruit?" Because if there was faith, then there will be fruit. Paul says Abraham's faith was credited to him as righteousness at the moment he believed. That leads us to ask questions like, "How do we know Abraham's faith was real?" And James tells us Abraham was willing to sacrifice his son in obedience to God. This can only be the fruit of faith. When Paul says, "For we conclude that a man is justified by faith apart from the works of the law" (Rom 3:28), he is saying a man is justified by wholehearted trust in the grace of Christ, not from any work he can do to earn his way to God. And James is in the background saying, "Amen!" And when James says, "You see that a man is justified by works and not by faith alone" (Jas 2:24), he is saying a man is not justified by a cold, intellectual belief in Jesus that even the demons have. Instead, a man is justified by a faith that produces radical obedience and sacrifice. And Paul is in the background saying, "Amen!" If this sounds confusing, we'll try to summarize everything with two truths below.

Two Truths to Remember

Two truths summarize everything we've seen so far. First, **salvation is through faith**. We are not saved through works; we are saved through faith. This is particularly what we saw in Paul: **Through initial faith in**

Christ, we are made right before God the Father. If you were to ask Paul or James, "How can I be saved?" they would both answer by saying that **Christ is the basis for our salvation**. James speaks of having "faith in our glorious Lord Jesus Christ" (2:1). Jesus has done the work. He has conquered sin, and He has purchased righteousness for us, so there is no work for us to do. His work on the cross and in the resurrection is the basis of our salvation. But how is that work applied to my life? The answer is this: **faith is the means of our salvation**. Trust in the person and work of Christ, and this is how you can be saved (Acts 16:31). Turn from yourself and trust in Him to save you from your sins and to be the Lord over your life, and you will be made right before God the Father. **This gives us radical confidence**. When God gives you birth through the word of truth (Jas 1:18), you don't ever have to fear anything in this life. You don't have to fear death itself because you are right before God the Father for all of eternity. Salvation is through faith.

The second truth to summarize this passage is that **faith works**. When Christ gives you spiritual birth, He gives you spiritual life— a life that is radically different and a life that bears great fruit. Look at Abraham: Yes, through His initial trust in God, He was made right before God the Father, but **through continual faith in Christ, we walk with God as friend**. An easy believism is rampant today in contemporary (so-called) Christianity where all kinds of people are claiming and believing they are right before God the Father, but they have absolutely no interest in walking with God as friend. And James says such people don't have faith; their faith is dead.

This picture of Abraham being called God's friend in James 2:23 is not an exact quote from the Old Testament although it is somewhat similar to descriptions of Abraham in 2 Chronicles 20:7 and Isaiah 41:8 (Moo, *James*, 139; Blomberg and Kamell, *James*, 138). Yet the picture is the same as what we hear from the mouth of Jesus when He says to His disciples in John 15:14, "You are My friends if you do what I command you." It is the natural overflow of knowing God as Father to enjoy God as friend. Such faith **results in radical obedience**. When your faith is in God as Father and as friend, then you do not need to be afraid to obey Him. You do not need to fear His commands. Even when He says to do things that make no sense to us or to the world around us, and even when He calls us to take steps that risk everything, we can obey. Why? Because **we trust God wholeheartedly**. This is why Abraham was willing to sacrifice his son: because he trusted God. And when we trust God, **we**

will follow God sacrificially. We'll sacrifice everything in obedience to His commands.

Reflect and Discuss

1. How would you respond to someone who says the Bible has many contradictions? How do you think through passages that seem to contradict one another?
2. How is James 2:20-24 consistent with Paul's teaching on justification by faith alone?
3. What's the difference between dead faith and living faith?
4. Explain this statement: We should differentiate between positional righteousness and practical righteousness, but we shouldn't completely separate them.
5. What's the difference between works God approves and works that are an affront to Him?
6. What's the danger of leaving the gospel out of a discussion on the works God requires?
7. What works or spiritual disciplines are you tempted to rely on for a right standing before God?
8. What's the difference between our initial justification and our justification on the last day?
9. What is the basis of your salvation? Why is it so crucial to know this truth?
10. What passages of Scripture would you point someone to in order to show them the kind of fruit God expects from His people?

Faith Risks

JAMES 2:25-26

Main Idea: As an example of faith and a recipient of scandalous grace, Rahab feared the sovereign God and risked everything for the spread of His glory.

I. **Radical Rahab (2:25-26)**
   A. She was a recipient of scandalous grace.
   B. She feared and revered the sovereign God.
   C. She risked it all for the spread of His glory.
   Excursus: Radical Action
II. **Summation of Justification**
   A. Three realities
      1. Christ is the basis of our justification.
      2. Faith is the means of our justification.
      3. Works are the evidence of our justification.
   B. Two reminders
      1. These realities are only possible by the grace of God.
      2. These realities are ultimately involved in judgment before God.

The theme of the second half of James 2 is captured in several verses:

Faith, if it doesn't have works, is dead by itself. (v. 17)

Are you willing to learn that faith without works is useless? (v. 20)

For just as the body without the spirit is dead, so also faith without works is dead. (v. 26)

We've seen Abraham used as an example of genuine faith that produces works. In verses 21-23 James tells us that Abraham was willing to sacrifice his only son because he had faith. Now in verse 25 James says, "And in the same way," which means he is not introducing a new truth. Rather, he is giving us another example of saving faith, and the example he uses is Rahab.

*And in the same way, wasn't Rahab the prostitute also justified
by works when she received the messengers and sent them out by a
different route? For just as the body without the spirit is dead, so also
faith without works is dead.* (James 2:25-26)

Radical Rahab
JAMES 2:25-26

The story of Abraham in Genesis 22 is familiar to most people, but this
may not be the case with Rahab, so we need to consider the context of
Joshua 2 for the setup to what James is saying. The people of God were
ready to take the promised land for the glory of God, and the first major
city in the land was Jericho. So Joshua decided to send some spies into
the land to scout things out.

*Joshua son of Nun secretly sent two men as spies from the Acacia
Grove, saying, "Go and scout the land, especially Jericho." So they left,
and they came to the house of a woman, a prostitute named Rahab,
and stayed there.*

*The king of Jericho was told, "Look, some of the Israelite men have
come here tonight to investigate the land." Then the king of Jericho
sent word to Rahab and said, "Bring out the men who came to you
and entered your house, for they came to investigate the entire land."*

*But the woman had taken the two men and hidden them. So she
said, "Yes, the men did come to me, but I didn't know where they were
from. At nightfall, when the gate was about to close, the men went out,
and I don't know where they were going. Chase after them quickly,
and you can catch up with them!" But she had taken them up to the
roof and hidden them among the stalks of flax that she had arranged
on the roof. The men pursued them along the road to the fords of the
Jordan, and as soon as they left to pursue them, the gate was shut.*

*Before the men fell asleep, she went up on the roof and said to
them, "I know that the LORD has given you this land and that the
terror of you has fallen on us, and everyone who lives in the land is
panicking because of you. For we have heard how the LORD dried up
the waters of the Red Sea before you when you came out of Egypt, and
what you did to Sihon and Og, the two Amorite kings you completely
destroyed across the Jordan. When we heard this, we lost heart, and*

everyone's courage failed because of you, for the LORD *your God is God in heaven above and on earth below. Now please swear to me by the* LORD *that you will also show kindness to my family, because I showed kindness to you. Give me a sure sign that you will spare the lives of my father, mother, brothers, sisters, and all who belong to them, and save us from death."*

The men answered her, "We will give our lives for yours. If you don't report our mission, we will show kindness and faithfulness to you when the LORD *gives us the land."*

Then she let them down by a rope through the window, since she lived in a house that was built into the wall of the city. "Go to the hill country so that the men pursuing you won't find you," she said to them. "Hide yourselves there for three days until they return; afterward, go on your way."

The men said to her, "We will be free from this oath you made us swear, unless, when we enter the land, you tie this scarlet cord to the window through which you let us down. Bring your father, mother, brothers, and all your father's family into your house. If anyone goes out the doors of your house, his blood will be on his own head, and we will be innocent. But if anyone with you in the house should be harmed, his blood will be on our heads. And if you report our mission, we are free from the oath you made us swear."

"Let it be as you say," she replied, and she sent them away. After they had gone, she tied the scarlet cord to the window.

So the two men went into the hill country and stayed there three days until the pursuers had returned. They searched all along the way, but did not find them. Then the men returned, came down from the hill country, and crossed the Jordan. They went to Joshua son of Nun and reported everything that had happened to them. They told Joshua, "The LORD *has handed over the entire land to us. Everyone who lives in the land is also panicking because of us."* (Josh 2:1-24)

Keep in mind that someone who served in Rahab's profession, if we can call it that, also served as an innkeeper of sorts. Her house was a common place for people to stay. The spies entered Rahab's house, and she protected them from death, so when the people of God took the city of Jericho in Joshua 6, she and her household were saved. So, why is James talking about this prostitute in the New Testament? There are three reasons.

She Was a Recipient of Scandalous Grace

Think about the contrast between Abraham and Rahab:

Abraham	Rahab
the patriarch of the Jewish people	a prostitute in the middle of a Gentile nation
the friend of God	living in the middle of the enemies of God
a great leader	a common citizen
at the top of the social order	at the bottom of the social order

You can hear the shock in James's voice in verse 25: Was not even Rahab *the prostitute* considered righteous? We're reminded of the genealogy in Matthew 1. Ruth, a Moabite woman grafted into the people of God in the Old Testament, is listed in the genealogy of Christ in the New Testament. However, according to Matthew 1:5, Rahab was Ruth's mother-in-law! What kind of family tree is this? God—the holy God of the universe—took a prostitute and brought her into His family, into the line that would lead to His Son. This is scandalous grace, and I don't mean in an immoral way, but grace that shocks by reaching down into the least likely of lives and pouring out mercy.

Praise be to God that He has reached down past our gross immorality, extended His arm across our filthy sinfulness, and brought us into His family. We are recipients of scandalous grace. This is the whole picture of justification. How can a holy God be just and yet include you in His family? By pouring out the just wrath due your sin upon His Son. God is just—He punishes sin to the fullest extent—and He justifies those who have faith in Jesus (Rom 3:26).

She Feared and Revered the Sovereign God

Remember what Rahab said to the spies: "When we heard this, we lost heart, and everyone's courage failed because of you, for the LORD your God is God in heaven above and on earth below" (Josh 2:11).

Now Rahab didn't have a lot of information; all she had was hearsay, stories she had heard about the people of God walking through the Red Sea on dry ground and being delivered by God against foreign armies. But the little bit she had heard, she believed. She knew Yahweh is God in heaven and on the earth. She knew He was sovereign over all things, and she knew she was accountable to Him. Rahab knew judgment was coming on her and her land, and she feared and revered the sovereign God. She was willing to take this risk, this radical step of obedience, because she believed God. And when you believe God, you are willing to risk everything.

She Risked It All for the Spread of God's Glory

If the king had discovered that these Jewish spies were in Rahab's home, she and her family would have been executed immediately. This was treason: Rahab's life was on the line. Like James, Hebrews points to Rahab as a hero of faith (Heb 11:31). But is she a hero of faith because of her rituals or religious activities? No, she is a hero of faith because she put her life and everything dear to her on the line for the Lord, trusting Him without hesitation, qualification, or reservation. She risked it all, going against everything in the culture around her. She risked it all so the people of God might take Jericho for the glory of God, and according to James she was considered righteous for what she did.

Are you willing to do that in your life? Are you willing to take risks in obedience to the Word of God because you revere the sovereign God who has saved you by His scandalous grace? Thousands of years after Abraham took his son to a mountain to sacrifice him, thousands of years after Rahab risked her life, are we today willing to risk it all? Will we go against the grain of the culture around us, even the Christian subculture that surrounds us? Are we willing to take some risks for the glory of God's name?

―――――――

Excursus: Radical Action

During our study of this portion of the book of James, the Lord did a surprising work in the church I pastor. When we came to James 2, we were confronted with this reality that those who have received mercy extend mercy. And we knew from James 1 that we didn't have the option just to hear this Word and not do something about it. I wrote about our church's response in the books *Radical* and *Radical Together.*

As we were studying James, we were going through our church budgeting process. To be honest, I hate budget season. As a pastor, I believe it's where the church comes face-to-face with how prone we are to give our resources to good things while ignoring great need. Christians in North America will give 2.5 percent of their income to their church this year (Empty Tomb, "Giving Research"). Out of that 2.5 percent, churches in North America will give 2 percent of their budgeted monies to needs overseas (Ronsvalle and Ronsvalle, *State*, 104). In other words, for every one hundred dollars a North American Christian makes, we will give five cents through the church to a world of urgent spiritual and physical need. This does not make sense.

Knowing this, one night our pastors took a hard look at the realities of the world, from the vast numbers of our brothers and sisters who are starving to the great multitudes of people who have never heard the gospel. Then we looked at our budget. And then we took action. We decided to change our spending drastically to align better with the will and ways of God.

This began with reallocating budget overages. Our staff had already been frugal, and we had saved more than $500,000 for the future. But James caused us to realize we had brothers and sisters around the world who already needed it. God began turning our eyes toward our brothers and sisters in India, a country that is home to 41 percent of the world's poor. Many children there do not even live to age five, so we looked for an avenue through which we could serve them. We learned that for about $25,000, we could provide food and water, medical care, and education to moms and their babies in a particular village for one year. We found 21 churches in impoverished villages across India, and we started thinking about which ones we might be able to serve. That's when we stepped back and realized, "If there are 21 churches in villages we can connect with, and in each one we can serve starving children and their families for about $25,000, that comes to a total of $525,000. Meanwhile, God has given us over $500,000." So we decided to give it all away.

Then we began looking at our 2010 budget. We decided to ask the staff to go through the budget with a fine-tooth comb and cut every expenditure we possibly could so we could give more around the world. When I sat down with our leaders, I tried to soften the blow of what cuts might mean for individual ministries. But as I was sharing, one of our preschool leaders spoke up. "David," she said, "you don't have to go soft on us. We realize from God's Word this is something we need to do, and it is something we want to do. So let us get to work and start cutting our budgets!"

With that said, we split up into different teams to reevaluate our budgets. What happened next was amazing. Whereas the budgeting process usually involves leaders vying with one another to see who can raise their budget the most, this year our leaders were competing with one another to see who could cut their budget the most. We soon saw that making cuts was not just going to affect our budgets as leaders but the lives of our members. So we believed it was important to have the entire church vote on moving forward in this direction, and that's what we did. We put a proposal before our church family that said the following:

> In love to God, in light of the needs around the world, and in obedience to Scripture (Prov 14:31; 21:13; 28:27; Matt 25:31-46; Jas 2:14-24; 1 John 3:16-18), the leadership of The Church at Brook Hills proposes that the church body affirm the following actions:
>
> • We will immediately begin radical saving as a church during the remainder of the year for the sake of urgent spiritual and physical need around the world.

- Our leadership will work together over the next two months on a budget that saves every expenditure possible for the sake of urgent spiritual and physical need around the world.
- We will immediately designate up to $525,000 of our current excess cash to serve impoverished churches across India.

A couple of weeks later, the church voted overwhelmingly in favor of reallocating resources in this direction. We were able to free up an additional $1.5 million from our next church budget. With that money we began to focus more on spreading the gospel in Birmingham and around the world.

Locally we identified an area of our city with particular needs, and we committed time and money to partner with other churches, organizations, and schools to share and show the gospel in tangible ways there. Not wanting to give our money without going ourselves, we challenged every member in our faith family to pray about possibly leaving their comfortable neighborhoods and moving into this area of the city. Since that time several individuals, couples, and families have done exactly that.

Globally we focused on northern India, home to 600 million people but where fewer than 0.5 percent are evangelical Christians. Based on relationships we already had and new partnerships we were able to form, we committed time and money to meeting urgent needs there. During the year through local Indian churches, we were able to provide food, education, medical care, and most importantly the gospel to more than a thousand families in extremely impoverished and unreached areas. In addition, we were able to work with other Indian churches to build a hundred wells that would provide clean water for tens of thousands who previously didn't have it. On top of these things, we were able to train hundreds of national church leaders, mobilize church planters to engage hundreds of villages for the first time with the good news of Christ, and give millions access to the Bible in their language for the first time.

My purpose in sharing these things is not to draw attention to the church I pastor. Anything we have done is merely evidence of God's grace among us. And we know that we have a long way to go. I share these things simply to encourage you to consider the possibilities of what might happen in your life and in your church when you put God's Word into practice. In light of James 2, let's continually put everything on the table before God in order that we might spend our lives and our resources intentionally and sacrificially for the glory of our King.

Summation of Justification

As we come to the close of James 2 and the discussion of what saving faith looks like, we need to consider what it means to be righteous before God.

Three Realities

Christ is the basis of our justification. How can you and I as sinners be declared right before God? We can't get rid of our sin, and we can't stand righteous before God on our own; there is nothing we can do. We need someone else who is righteous to be righteousness for us. And this is what the gospel is all about. Jesus lived a righteous life in our place, and then He died the death that we deserve. Second Corinthians 5:21 says, "[God] made [Christ] who did not know sin to be sin for us, so that we might become the righteousness of God in [Christ]." Christ's work is the basis of our justification. So if someone asks you, "How do you know that you are right before God?" and the first words out of your mouth are "Because I have done _____," then you are missing the point of the gospel. You can only be right before God because Christ lived the life you could not live and died the death you deserved to die. This is the starting point.

Now the question becomes, How is Christ's work applied to your life? Is it automatic, so that when He died, everyone was saved automatically?

Is it something you are born into? Or is there something you have to do? This question leads us to the second reality concerning how we become righteous before God.

Faith is the means of our justification. Faith is the antiwork. It is trust. It is surrender. It is the realization that you can do nothing but trust in what has been done for you. And through faith you are united to Jesus, being clothed and credited with His righteousness. However, such faith is not mere intellectual assent. Faith is not merely, "Yes, Jesus died on a cross." Demons believe that, and they don't have faith. Faith, according to Scripture, means turning from yourself and trusting in Jesus as your Savior from sin and as the Lord of your life. It's the moment when God opens your eyes to see His glory, to see your need, and to see His provision, and in faith you confess your need for Christ and you submit your life to Him. This is faith, and in the words of Paul in Romans 5:1, "Therefore, since we have been declared righteous by faith, we have peace with God through our Lord Jesus Christ." Justification happens in an instant, but the faith by which we are justified changes everything about us, and this is the point of James's letter.

Works are the evidence of our justification because faith bears fruit. Does that mean our works are now the basis of our justification? Absolutely not. Our works (not works fueled by the flesh that don't honor God but works that are the fruit of faith and bring great glory to God) are the evidence that we have been justified. Abraham believed God, and consequently he was willing to sacrifice his son. Rahab believed God, and consequently she was willing to risk it all. In these two examples from James 2, Abraham and Rahab showed their faith by what they did.

Two Reminders

These realities are only possible by the grace of God. God's grace not only draws us to faith while we are dead in our sins, but even after this our obedience is fueled by God's grace. Both our faith and our works are made possible by God. All is of grace. As an analogy, imagine giving money to one of your children for them to buy you a Christmas present. They give you the present, but did they really? Sure, in a sense it came from you, but it was also an expression of their love for you. The illustration is not perfect, but it does help us see that anything we bring to God as an offering that is pleasing to Him is an overflow of His grace. I think this is one of the reasons James chooses, of all people, Rahab as an example of faith. In this picture of a prostitute, he wants to make sure we're not talking about merit we bring to God—our own righteousness. No, we're talking about the grace of God alive in the risk-taking obedience of a woman. By grace we are saved through faith (Eph 2:8). *These realities are ultimately involved in the judgment before God.* The judgment refers to the time when you stand before God in heaven. We're talking about final justification, the time when your eternal destiny will be declared openly and finally. What will be the *basis* by which you enter into heaven to dwell in the presence of God for all of eternity? Christ. The only way we can go to heaven is on the basis of Christ. And what is the *means* by which you will be declared right on that day for all of eternity? Faith. The faith that says, "Father, I have nothing in me to stand on. I trust wholly in the righteousness of Christ to stand for me. You opened my eyes to Your holiness and my sin, and You opened my eyes to Christ as my Savior and my Lord. By grace you did this, and faith is the means." In the background of your life on that final day, it will be evident whether such faith was indeed a reality in your life. What Paul said is true:

> *[God] will repay each one according to his works.* (Rom 2:6)

> *For we must all appear before the tribunal of Christ, so that each may be repaid for what he has done in the body, whether good or worthless.* (2 Cor 5:10)

If there is no fruit of real faith on the last day, and the only thing you have to lean on is a card you signed or a prayer you prayed, or even religious rituals in which you participated, then it will be shown clearly that you never really had faith at all. And you will miss eternal life and be cast away to eternal death.

I do not desire to be a hellfire and damnation preacher, but even more so I do not want people to be deceived. It grieves my heart when people die in my own community, people with no fruit of faith in Christ, and yet our church-filled community concludes that surely they are with God in heaven. It's not true. Now, to be clear, none of us knows the inner secrets of a person's heart, nor are we the final judge. But God's Word is clear: any claim to faith with no resultant fruit is like a dead corpse. There's no life there. Instead, there's death in hell for all eternity.

Therefore, if you have not truly believed in Jesus Christ for salvation, I urge you to do so today. Look to Christ crucified as the only basis by which you can be declared righteous. By God's grace admit your need for Christ and trust in Him. Do not give mere intellectual assent or perform a religious exercise. Cast yourself in faith on Christ. For when you do that, the God of the universe will look down on your sinful heart and save you. He will clothe you in the righteousness of Christ and you will have peace with God. And through such faith, Christ will come into your life and change it from the inside out, for your good and for His glory. He will transform your life into one that demonstrates His grace and love and mercy to the world around you. This is the faith that saves, and this is a faith that works.

Reflect and Discuss

1. How does the free nature of God's grace give us hope as we encounter people of all different walks of life?
2. Explain why Rahab's actions didn't earn her favor with God.
3. How did Rahab's actions give evidence of saving faith?
4. How is Rahab a picture of every follower of Christ, no matter their testimony?
5. Why is reverence for God so crucial to our faith?
6. What does risking it all look like in your life?
7. What do we mean when we say faith is the means of our justification? How is this different from the basis of our justification?
8. How is it that even our faith is a result of God's grace?
9. If justification is by faith, how do our works factor into the day of judgment?
10. How does focusing on trusting in the basis of our justification (Christ and His finished work) free us and motivate us to do good works?

Faith Speaks[13]

JAMES 3:1-12

Main Idea: We need to recognize that the tongue is untamable, capable of great damage, and an indicator of our hearts, but God has a gracious provision in the gospel for our sinful words.

I. **God Speaks.**
   A. Recognize the importance of words.
II. **Satan Speaks.**
   A. Recognize the cunning and deceptive words of the serpent.
III. **People Speak.**
   A. Recognize the great responsibility of teaching God's Word (3:1).
   B. Recognize the great potential of sinning in what we say (3:2).
   C. Recognize the great power of the tongue (3:3-6).
   D. Recognize our inability to tame the tongue (3:7-10).
   E. Recognize that our words are an indication of our hearts (3:11-12).
IV. **God Speaks to the Fallen, the Dying, and the Hopeless.**
   A. Recognize God's provision for the imperfect words we have spoken and the imperfect words we have believed.
V. **The Church Speaks.**
   A. Recognize our responsibility to speak the truth in love to one another.
   B. Recognize our responsibility to take this gospel (good news!) to our neighbors and to the nations.

As followers of Christ, we are those who have found life, hope, and deep joy in knowing God. He has saved us from our sin, and we have been forever changed. James knows how we feel. James, the half brother of Jesus, wrote this letter close to two thousand years ago. He knew what it was like to experience the power of the cross. I wonder how many times as a young man James sinned against his older half brother

---

[13] This section is based on a sermon by Deric Thomas.

Jesus. I wonder how many times he spoke to Him sinfully and wrongly complained about Him to Mary. We know that it was later when James actually recognized Jesus for who He really was. After having seen Jesus die on the cross and then appear after His resurrection, James likely reflected many times on his life growing up with Jesus.

As a pastor in the early church, James writes to a group of Christians, most of whom were probably Jewish, to talk to them about the power and importance of words, words that flow from the tongue or, even more fundamentally, from the heart. Jesus made clear where our words come from when He said in Luke 6:45 that we speak "from the overflow of the heart." We all know words are critically important. We have all been deeply hurt by words, and we have also been greatly helped, encouraged, and blessed through words. In James 3:1-12 we'll see what James (under the inspiration of the Holy Spirit) has to say about our words and the way we use our tongue.

I had to travel a lot for one of my first full-time jobs after college. My first major trip that I can remember was to Dallas, Texas. I remember booking my flight, my hotel room, and my car rental, and I was ready to go. I showed up in Dallas, got off the plane and into my car, and I hit the interstate. If you have ever been to Dallas, you know how complicated it can be to get on the interstate and find your destination. As I was riding out of the airport, I realized one major problem: I didn't have directions to the hotel. Since this was my first big trip, I had overlooked one small thing (or maybe it was a big thing!). If you are in Dallas, Texas, on the interstate without directions, you are in bad shape.

So often this is how we are in life as well. We find ourselves living at 70 mph, driving full speed ahead, but not really knowing where we are going. But it does not have to be this way because God has spoken. He has given us His Word that teaches us and shows us the way to go as we follow our Lord and Savior Jesus Christ. Before we see what James says about the tongue, let's take a little glimpse at what the Bible says to us about words. We'll do a biblical theology on this theme, beginning with Genesis 1:3 where God speaks.

God Speaks

Genesis 1:3 says, "Then God said, 'Let there be light.'" This little phrase, "Then God said," comes before each thing God creates, even before He creates humanity. God created all things by the power of words, by His Word! Therefore, we need to **recognize the importance of words**. That

God uses words to create demonstrates their importance (Gen 1:3; Ps 33:6-9; Heb 11:3).

God uses words not only to create but also to reveal Himself. Consider Genesis 1:27-28:

> *So God created man in His own image;*
> *He created him in the image of God;*
> *He created them male and female.*
> *God blessed them, and God said to them, "Be fruitful, multiply,*
> *fill the earth, and subdue it. Rule the fish of the sea, the birds of the*
> *sky, and every creature that crawls on the earth."*

God gives Adam and Eve their purpose for existing. Humans, even before the fall and the effects of sin, needed a voice outside themselves to tell them what they were created to do. God is the One who revealed to them their purpose. They were to have babies and rule the world! Not only that, God also gave them the ability to speak to Him in praise and worship and relationship and to speak to each other in relationship. Notice too in Genesis 2:16-17 that God gave them commands through His words:

> *And the LORD God commanded the man, "You are free to eat from any*
> *tree of the garden, but you must not eat from the tree of the knowledge*
> *of good and evil, for on the day you eat from it, you will certainly die."*

God highly values His words, and He highly values our words as well. God reveals Himself by words spoken and written (Gen 1:27-28; 2:16; 12:1; 2 Tim 3:16). Not only that, God also speaks to Himself. That may sound strange since God is One (Deut 6:4), but God is also three. There is only one true and living God, but the glorious doctrine of the Holy Trinity found in God's revealed Word teaches us that God is one in essence and three in persons. Genesis 1:26 speaks to this reality:

> *Then God said, "Let Us make man in Our image, according to Our*
> *likeness. They will rule the fish of the sea, the birds of the sky, the*
> *livestock, all the earth, and the creatures that crawl on the earth."*

Notice the words "Us" and "Our," which seem to indicate that more than one person is in view. The New Testament further explains God's speaking to Himself. We see in John 15:15 that the Father speaks to the Son, and then the Son teaches the disciples. Jesus speaks of "everything I have heard from My Father," which He hears and then shares verbally with the disciples. Or think of John 17:1 when Jesus speaks to the Father in prayer: "Jesus spoke these things, looked up to heaven, and said: 'Father, the hour has come. Glorify Your Son so that the Son may glorify You.'" God clearly speaks to Himself, and this truth makes words important.[14] But God isn't the only one who speaks.

Satan Speaks

Satan also speaks. In Genesis 3:1 we read,

> *Now the serpent was the most cunning of all the wild animals that the LORD God had made. He said to the woman, "Did God really say, 'You can't eat from any tree in the garden'?"*

We must **recognize the cunning and deceptive words of the serpent**. Satan's words contradict, distort, and twist God's Word. Look also at Genesis 3:4-5:

> *"No! You will not die," the serpent said to the woman. "In fact, God knows that when you eat it your eyes will be opened and you will be like God, knowing good and evil."*

Words are so important, not only because they can be used in many good ways but also because they can be used in many evil ways. This brings us to James 3 where we see that not only God and Satan speak, but also people speak.

People Speak

Recognize the Great Responsibility of Teaching God's Word (3:1)

Beginning with James 3:1, we learn that we need to recognize the great responsibility of teaching God's Word. James says, "Not many should become teachers, my brothers, knowing that we will receive a stricter judgment." James warns his readers that great care and great prayer must go into becoming a teacher of God's Word. In this passage he is particularly talking about those who are called to the task of teaching God's Word in an official capacity as a leader in the church. But there is also a sense in which all of us as followers of Christ are teachers of God's

---

[14] See also Psalm 2:7-9 for another example of God speaking to Himself.

Word. Think of the Great Commission, where we are commanded to
"make disciples of all nations" (Matt 28:19), and to paraphrase the next
verse, "Teach those we disciple to observe all that Jesus has commanded
us."

Teaching God's Word is to be taken seriously because it is such a
great responsibility, and those who teach the Word will be judged with
greater strictness (Jas 3:2). When they stand before Christ, even as His
children, they will be judged for every word they have said. Jesus made
this clear in Matthew 12:36-37:

> *I tell you that on the day of judgment people will have to account for
> every careless word they speak. For by your words you will be acquitted,
> and by your words you will be condemned.*

False teachers who speak lies and distort the Word of God cunningly and
deceptively, like Satan, will be condemned to hell. For those who are in
Christ, our words also have eternal significance, for Christ Himself will
reward our faithfulness, and this will be based in part on the words we
have spoken. James is saying to the church, "Think of the eternal rami-
fications before you teach God's Word." God's Word alone is what we
should teach (2 Tim 4:1-2; 2:15).

Recognize the Great Potential of Sinning in What We Say (3:2)

The reason James considers it so important to note the eternal ramifica-
tions of our words is so we will recognize the great potential of sinning
in what we say. Every human being—including great Christian leaders
and teachers like James himself (notice his use of "we")—sins in many
ways. In fact, James says only the perfect, or fully mature, don't sin in
what they say (v. 2). Think of the way Romans 3:13-14 speaks of the
depravity of man as it relates to his speech:

> *Their throat is an open grave;*
> *they deceive with their tongues.*
> *Vipers' venom is under their lips.*
> *Their mouth is full of cursing and bitterness.*

Those who do not know God have tongues that are like open graves
filled with smelly, rotting, dead bodies. They use their tongues to lie
and to deceive people. They have snake venom spitting from under
their lips. They curse people and speak words of bitterness. This is not a
pretty picture God's Word is painting of the tongue.

This word "mature" in verse 2—*telos* in the Greek—can mean "complete, mature, or perfect." A mature Christian man or woman probably has learned to bridle his or her tongue to some degree. After all, James makes clear in 1:26 that any man who does not bridle his tongue has a worthless religion. However, James seems to be thinking of sinless perfection here. The man who is able to bridle his tongue perfectly would also be able to "control his whole body" (3:2), i.e., refrain from all other sins. No part of us is in a more slippery place than the tongue. I think that's why God has given us teeth and a mouth—teeth to cage in that deadly weapon, and a mouth to close it in.

Recognize the Great Power of the Tongue (3:3-6)

James says we all stumble in many ways, and this is seen particularly with regard to the sins of the tongue (see Rom 3:13-14,23). First, he tells us we need to recognize the great power of the tongue in verses 3-6. He gives three illustrations to hammer this point home. He says in verse 3, "Now when we put bits into the mouths of horses to make them obey us, we also guide the whole animal." My wife and I lived in Louisville while I was in seminary, and one of the part-time jobs I had during my first year of school was at an assisted living home called Atria. I was the assistant activities director, where I basically learned to play a mean game of bingo and to drive the elderly (whom I loved) to all the activities they enjoyed doing, like dancing and watching horse races at Churchill Downs (and no, I never gambled). It was captivating to watch those beautiful, strong, fast horses glide around that track with such precision as they were ridden by those rather short men on their backs. At the time I did not think about how that little bit in the horse's mouth was used to guide and direct such a large animal. This is James's point in verse 3: by controlling the mouth of a strong horse, we can control his whole body.

James then goes on to mention a ship as his next example in verse 4: "And consider ships: Though very large and driven by fierce winds, they are guided by a very small rudder wherever the will of the pilot directs." When I lived in Miami, Florida, I remember driving down by the coast and seeing huge harbors filled with Carnival cruise ships. I never got to ride on one, but it is amazing how one of those boats can be guided out of the harbor, onto the sea, and to its destination by such a small rudder on the stern. All the captain does is turn the wheel, and the rudder shifts from one way to the other, and then the entire ship follows. Something as small as a rudder can control something as large as a Carnival cruise ship. And that is James's point: something as small as the tongue can have a huge impact on our entire lives, and the lives of others. The last of James's three illustrations comes in verse 5, and it has to do with a spark and a fire: "So too, though the tongue is a small part of the body, it boasts great things. Consider how large a forest a small fire ignites." Water does not spread rapidly; it stays where it falls. But not fire. If you drop a spark in the right place, like a dry forest, then you could have a blazing inferno on your hands in a matter of moments because fire multiplies fast. A small spark can start a large fire. Notice what Proverbs says about people's tongues:

> *A worthless man digs up evil, and his speech is like a scorching fire.* (Prov 16:27)

> *As charcoal for embers and wood for fire, so is a quarrelsome man for kindling strife.* (Prov 26:21)

Show me a man or woman who stirs up strife, who is a gossip, or who criticizes everything due to a proud and critical heart, and I will show you someone who has hurt many people in their path, starting in their own home. Think of ways the words of people have affected you positively and negatively (see Jas 1:19). Words hurt, and many of us have been affected deeply by them. In fact, some of us have never gotten over what someone said to us in the past. Many still carry the wounds from those hateful, evil, satanic words. "Satanic?" you ask. Yes, satanic. In verse 6 James says that the tongue is actually "set on fire by hell." The word "hell" in verse 6 is the word *gehenna* in Greek. It is a reference to the place right outside of Jerusalem where trash was burned around the clock. During and after Old Testament times, pagan peoples would sacrifice their children at this location, which is also called the Valley of Hinnom. Jesus used the word *gehenna* as a reference to hell itself, the place where the wicked would spend eternity and the place that was prepared for Satan and his demons. The tongue is a dangerous weapon! That is probably why James told us earlier in 1:19 that we are to be "quick to hear, slow to speak, and slow to anger."

Recognize Our Inability to Tame the Tongue (3:7-10)

You must recognize the danger of the tongue, and you must recognize our inability to tame the tongue. This is brought out clearly in verses

7-10. Humans can tame all kinds of animals. Some dogs obey better than some children. I remember living in Miami and going to the Miami Sea Aquarium to watch the big orca (whale) that had been tamed by trainers to do all kinds of amazing tricks. It's amazing that we can train something so huge but that no human being can tame the tongue! The tongue, James says, is a "restless evil, full of deadly poison" (v. 8). We use the tongue to bless God, and then on the other hand we use it to curse people (vv. 9-10).

I have learned over my Christian life that it is pretty easy to fool people. We can seem so nice, gentle, loving, and kind in public, but our families or our closest friends know who we really are. The truth is we are all in bad shape if we are left to ourselves. Despite the advice of many self-help books and so-called experts today, we cannot change ourselves, and that includes our speech. No man can tame the tongue because our problems are deeper than our mouths.

Recognize That Our Words Are an Indication of Our Hearts (3:11-12)

On your own you are in a helpless predicament, and you need to recognize that your words are an indication of your heart and therefore of your true spiritual condition (see Jer 13:23; Mark 10:25-27). In 3:11-12 James uses several illustrations: fresh water springs don't produce salt water; fig trees don't produce olives; a grapevine does not produce figs; a salt pond can't yield fresh water. Sinful words inevitably come from a sinful heart. Our problems are deeper than most people think. Consider Mark 7:14-23:

> *Summoning the crowd again, He told them, "Listen to Me, all of you, and understand: Nothing that goes into a person from outside can defile him, but the things that come out of a person are what defile him. If anyone has ears to hear, he should listen!"*
>
> *When He went into the house away from the crowd, the disciples asked Him about the parable. And He said to them, "Are you also as lacking in understanding? Don't you realize that nothing going into a man from the outside can defile him? For it doesn't go into his heart but into the stomach and is eliminated." (As a result, He made all foods clean.) Then He said, "What comes out of a person—that defiles him. For from within, out of people's hearts, come evil thoughts, sexual immoralities, thefts, murders, adulteries, greed, evil actions, deceit,*

promiscuity, stinginess, blasphemy, pride, and foolishness. All these evil things come from within and defile a person. "

Words that are evil, immoral, deceitful, hateful, adulterous, wicked, sensual, slanderous, proud, and foolish come from within. They come from the heart, and that is a deeper problem than the mouth. Jesus is not talking about the heart as the organ in your chest. It is the real you, the core of who you are. He says something similar in Luke 6:43-49:

A good tree doesn't produce bad fruit; on the other hand, a bad tree doesn't produce good fruit. For each tree is known by its own fruit. Figs aren't gathered from thornbushes, or grapes picked from a bramble bush. A good man produces good out of the good storeroom of his heart. An evil man produces evil out of the evil storeroom, for his mouth speaks from the overflow of the heart.

Why do you call Me "Lord, Lord," and don't do the things I say? I will show you what someone is like who comes to Me, hears My words, and acts on them: He is like a man building a house, who dug deep and laid the foundation on the rock. When the flood came, the river crashed against that house and couldn't shake it, because it was well built. But the one who hears and does not act is like a man who built a house on the ground without a foundation. The river crashed against it, and immediately it collapsed. And the destruction of that house was great!

Imagine a man who has an apple tree in his backyard that only produces rotten apples. He really wants it to produce delicious, red apples in order to make an apple pie, but all he gets is rotten fruit. Then he tells you he has a plan to fix the tree, and you see him come home from the grocery store the next day with a big bag of shiny red apples. He gets out his heavy-duty nail gun and starts stapling these good apples to the tree. The tree is alive and healthy, right? Wrong.

The fruit on the tree may look good from a distance, but there's still a problem with the root. So it is with us: our hearts, and not just our behavior and our speech, are bad apart from Christ. So much of what we read and hear about in terms of people changing and growing spiritually is nothing more than fruit stapling. When our children use bad language, we tell them to talk better. That's certainly necessary, but we've got to address the problem at a deeper level. Jesus tells us that our tongue problems are heart problems. We don't need a spiritual tongue doctor but a spiritual cardiologist. And, praise God, we have one.

God Speaks to the Fallen, the Dying, and the Hopeless

All of us are guilty of sinning with our words, and if we're honest, James's warnings can leave us feeling condemned. But this is where I want to encourage you, in light of your sin, to **recognize God's provision for the imperfect words we have spoken and the imperfect words we have believed**. God speaks in creation, Satan speaks in the fall, but then God speaks again in redemption. And God has the last word! He has revealed a word of gospel promise. All of us have been burned by broken promises, and we have even burned others by broken promises of all kinds. But God always keeps His promises. Therefore, no matter how the words of other people and their broken promises have affected you, as you learn to hear God's voice above all other voices, you can find hope and healing.

In the beginning, right after the fall, we read in Genesis 3:15 that God promised to send a baby, a child, the seed of the woman, and that this child would crush the head of the serpent—the enemies of God: Satan, sin, death, hell, and the grave. God kept this promise by sending His only Son, born of a woman, born under the law, to redeem those who had broken His law (Gal 4:4-5). Jesus came and lived the perfect life we could not live. He spoke the perfect words all of us have fallen short of, and He died in our place for our sinful words and actions. And then He was raised from the dead! The death that results from our sinful words has been overcome by the Word made flesh.

God has revealed His word of gospel wisdom, which is the wisdom we all need. James 3:13-18 describes what this wisdom ought to look like in our lives:

> *Who is wise and has understanding among you? He should show his works by good conduct with wisdom's gentleness. But if you have bitter envy and selfish ambition in your heart, don't brag and deny the truth. Such wisdom does not come from above but is earthly, unspiritual, demonic. For where envy and selfish ambition exist, there is disorder and every kind of evil. But the wisdom from above is first pure, then peace-loving, gentle, compliant, full of mercy and good fruits, without favoritism and hypocrisy. And the fruit of righteousness is sown in peace by those who cultivate peace.*

James talks about the "wisdom from above." The question is not, *What* is this wisdom? but *Who* is this Wisdom? First Corinthians 1:24 says that Christ is the wisdom of God. Similarly, 1 Corinthians 1:30 says that Christ became wisdom for us. As our substitute on the cross, our foolish words and their consequences were all imputed to Him, and His righteous words, His wisdom, was imputed to us. Colossians 2:2-3 says that all the treasures of wisdom and knowledge are found in Christ! John tells us that Jesus is the eternal Word who came from heaven to earth (John 1:1,14). Gaining wisdom is ultimately about knowing Him.

The Word of God is the ultimate solution to our word problem. And God always has the final word! James 1:18 makes clear that He saves sinners by the "message of truth." In other words, regeneration (being born again) happens through His Word. Death does not have the final word for God's people because on the cross Jesus defeated death for us and took on God's wrath in our place. He cried out, "It is finished!" (John 19:30). When Jesus returns, He will consummate His kingdom and will have the last word. This is the testimony of Revelation 21:5-7, where we learn that we will be sons of God for eternity in a new heaven and a new earth:

> Then the One seated on the throne said, "Look! I am making everything new." He also said, "Write, because these words are faithful and true." And He said to me, "It is done! I am the Alpha and the Omega, the Beginning and the End. I will give water as a gift to the thirsty from the spring of life. The victor will inherit these things, and I will be his God, and he will be My son.

The Church Speaks

So how do we respond to such powerful words from God? He has spoken so beautifully, and now the church speaks. We **recognize our responsibility to speak the truth in love to one another**. Each part of the body of Christ needs the other parts to grow to maturity (see Eph 4:11-16). We need to love one another in word and deed, and we need to do this in biblical community for the glory of God.

While we grow up together as the body of Christ, we need to **recognize our responsibility to take this gospel (good news!) to our neighbors and to the nations**. The prophet Isaiah's life was changed when he saw God in His holiness and recognized his own sinful lips and speech. He saw that God alone could cleanse his lips and his life (Isa 6:1-8). As a result, Isaiah was ready to go wherever God would send him. "Here I am. Send me," was his cry. God's response was clear: "Go! *Say* to these people . . ." (emphasis added). In other words, "Go and *speak* words of life!"

Is this your cry? Have you surrendered your life today to going and speaking His gospel? How will they hear if we don't open our mouths? Romans 10:14-17 makes clear that if we don't open our mouths, people will not hear, and if they do not hear the word of Christ, they will not be saved.

Reflect and Discuss

1. Recall a time when you've hurt someone with your words. What was motivating you?
2. What's wrong with the idea that our actions, and not our words, are what really matter?
3. The God of the Bible is the God who speaks. How should that reality affect our view of words, including our own?
4. Explain why the potential for great damage is so great in the case of teachers.
5. What are some characteristics we should look for in teachers of God's Word?
6. What do our words tell us about our hearts? Why is the tongue so difficult to control?
7. How would you counsel another believer whose conversation is often impure?
8. What are two or three practical ways you can be more careful with your words?
9. How do James's instructions apply to social media—texts, e-mails, Internet communication, etc.?
10. What should we expect from unbelievers in terms of their words? Explain your answer.

Faith Submits

JAMES 3:13–4:12

Main Idea: In His grace God works in us so that we pursue friendship with Him rather than friendship with the world, for worldly wisdom and speech are selfish and satanic.

I. **Two Pictures of Wisdom**
   A. Worldly wisdom (3:13-16)
      1. comes from hell,
      2. is motivated by self-centered ambition,
      3. and results in disorder and evil.
   B. Godly wisdom (3:17-18)
      1. comes from heaven,
      2. is motivated by God-centered humility,
      3. and results in peace and righteousness.
II. **Two Pictures of Friendship**
   A. Friendship with the world (4:1-5)
      1. comes from the sinful desires of the flesh,
      2. is motivated by a longing for earthly pleasure,
      3. and results in spiritual adultery against God.
   B. Friendship with God (4:6-10)
      1. comes from the gracious desire of God,
      2. is motivated by a longing for eternal satisfaction,
      3. and results in submission to the authority of God.
III. **Two Pictures of Speech (4:11-12)**
   A. Worldly speech
      1. discourages one another
      2. and dishonors God.
   B. Godly speech
      1. encourages one another
      2. and exalts God.
IV. **One Prayer in Faith**

As we walk with God in faith on a day-to-day basis, we face many challenges, trials, and temptations. For this reason James addresses issues of wisdom, friendship, and speech, showing how faith in Christ inevitably affects ordinary, everyday life in this world.

Two Pictures of Wisdom

James tells us in this passage that there are two sources of wisdom, and we need to be discerning as to where our wisdom comes from. A kind of wisdom comes from God, is pleasing to Him, and good for our lives. Another kind of wisdom does not come from God and is not good for our lives or for others' lives. After his introductory statement about "wisdom's gentleness" in verse 13, James starts with worldly wisdom.

Worldly Wisdom (3:13-16)

There is a wisdom that **comes from hell**. It's of the Devil. Yes, it's a worldly wisdom—it's earthly—but the problem goes even deeper than the earth. This kind of wisdom is the complete antithesis of anything that is from God. It is subtly yet powerfully demonic. In Genesis 3 the serpent tempted Eve to trust in his wisdom instead of God's wisdom, and the adversary is doing the same thing in every one of our lives today.

This is where we need to remember one of the most important factors in our growth in wisdom: our perspective. Worldly wisdom views life from a limited perspective. It doesn't see things in light of eternity but in terms of the perceived immediate impact—what is best for self-advancement and self-pleasure now. This is dangerous, and it **is motivated by self-centered ambition**. A wisdom in the world measures everything by how it affects you. It's concerned with how you can advance yourself, promote yourself, or assert yourself. When looking at conversations and circumstances, the question at the forefront is always, What can I get out of this? James says this is from the Devil. Remember the favoritism James confronted in chapter 2, a favoritism that was driven by nothing but self-centered ambition. People were ignoring the poor because they could not get anything from them. This kind of wisdom is common in the world, and it is common in us, yet we don't even see it.

Is self-centered ambition not the root of struggles in marriage? "What is best for me?" is the question we ask. Is this not the root of the entire American dream—climb the ladder, achieve your aspirations, assert yourself, promote yourself, advance yourself? Meanwhile, Jesus says, "Deny yourself." Self-centered ambition is at the heart of worldly wisdom, and it is demonic. It is filled with envy, always comparing itself to others to see who is better or worse. James says this **results in disorder and evil** (v. 16). In a home that is marked by self-centered ambition, you will have disorder and evil. In a church that is filled with men and women driven by self-centered ambition, you have a recipe for disorder and evil. There is a danger in all of our families and our churches whenever we pursue selfish concerns or partisan causes to the neglect of the good of others, and so we need to be on guard. Such wisdom produces anger, bitterness, resentment, divisions, and divorce. Such wisdom robs us of love, intimacy, trust, fellowship, and harmony with others.

Godly Wisdom (3:17-18)

What we need is godly wisdom that **comes from heaven**. This takes us back to James 1:5-6: "Now if any of you lacks wisdom, he should ask God, who gives to all generously and without criticizing, and it will be given to him." You don't get this wisdom from intellectual effort or practical experience as much as you get it from being with God. A kind of wisdom, a godly wisdom, sees things from an eternal perspective that can only come from God. We must go to Him constantly in prayer and in the Word, crying out to Him in order to receive His wisdom. This is the point of Proverbs 2:1-8:

> My son, if you accept my words
> and store up my commands within you,
>   listening closely to wisdom
> and directing your heart to understanding;
>   furthermore, if you call out to insight
> and lift your voice to understanding,
>   if you seek it like silver
> and search for it like hidden treasure,
>   then you will understand the fear of the LORD
> and discover the knowledge of God.
>   For the LORD gives wisdom;
> from His mouth come knowledge and understanding.
>   He stores up success for the upright;
> He is a shield for those who live with integrity
>   so that He may guard the paths of justice
> and protect the way of His loyal followers.

Individually and corporately, we need to go before God and pray for wisdom. We ought to be desperate for it. All believers should have the attitude of Solomon in 1 Kings 3, who confessed that he was but a child and in need of God's help (1 Kgs 3:7-9). Only God can give this wisdom, which is why godly wisdom **is motivated by God-centered humility**. In verses 17-18 James says, "But the wisdom from above is first pure, then peace-loving, gentle, compliant, full of mercy and good fruits, without favoritism and hypocrisy. And the fruit of righteousness is sown in peace by those who cultivate peace." Consider how these characterizations of wisdom in James are evident in the Beatitudes in Jesus' Sermon on the Mount in Matthew 5:3-12:

- Pure: "The pure in heart are blessed, for they will see God" (Matt 5:8).
- Peace-loving: "The peacemakers are blessed, for they will be called sons of God" (Matt 5:9).
- Gentle/Considerate: "The gentle are blessed, for they will inherit the earth" (Matt 5:5).
- Compliant/Submissive: "The poor in spirit are blessed, for the kingdom of heaven is theirs" (Matt 5:3).
- Full of mercy: "The merciful are blessed, for they will be shown mercy" (Matt 5:7).
- Full of good fruit: "Those who hunger and thirst for righteousness are blessed, for they will be filled" (Matt 5:6).

When you read James 3:17 in the original language, you see that James has organized these characteristics of wisdom in a beautiful literary style. They are grouped by the way they sound, and the result is a beautiful picture of the blessing of the wisdom that comes from God (Blomberg and Kamell, *James*, 175). This wisdom is God-centered— "The pure in heart are blessed, for they will see God" (Matt 5:8)—not self-centered. It's also humble, which is what James means in 3:13 when he refers to wisdom's "gentleness." Wisdom from God produces humility in man. But the world is exactly the opposite: Wisdom from the world produces self-centered pride in man.

In contrast to the disorder and evil that result from selfish ambition, James says in verse 18 that the wisdom from God **results in peace and righteousness**. God's wisdom produces that which is right, that which is pleasing and honoring to God, and that which is good for the people of God. "The peacemakers are blessed, for they will be called sons of God" (Matt 5:9). Peace is what God desires in our relationships, our homes, and our churches. Now this is not peace at the expense of truth, as in "let's just all get along" by avoiding truth and conviction. No, it's first of all "pure" (v. 17) and true, trusting that purity produces peace.

Think about how the peace James talks about plays out in your home. When a husband and wife are humbly going before God and pursuing wisdom that is pure and honoring to God, it produces peace in that home. This also happens in the church. When men and women are humbly going before God, leaving self-centered ambition behind and pursuing wisdom that is pure, it produces peacemaking and righteousness in that church. It doesn't mean you always agree on every single detail, but it does mean that together you are humbly seeking God's wisdom and putting aside selfish ambition.

We need to ask God to remove from us worldly thinking and worldly wisdom. Humble yourself before Him and ask Him to give you wisdom that is "first pure, then peace-loving, gentle, compliant, full of mercy and good fruits, without favoritism and hypocrisy" (v. 17). And pray that He would use you to sow not disorder and evil but to harvest peace and righteousness in your relationships with others.

Two Pictures of Friendship

We have a chapter break after 3:18, but the reality is that the fights and quarrels James refers to in chapter 4 flow from the worldly wisdom that was permeating the community of faith in chapter 3. In fact, the word "covet" in 4:2 comes from the same word James uses in 3:14 and 3:16 that is translated "envy." James illustrates in chapter 4 the disorder and evil that is the result of the envy and selfish ambition of chapter 3. This picture is summed up in 4:4: "Adulteresses! Don't you know that friendship with the world is hostility toward God? So whoever wants to be the world's friend becomes God's enemy." We've seen two pictures of wisdom that lead us now to think about two pictures of friendship.

Friendship with the World (4:1-5)

First we'll consider friendship with the world, which is what we should be fighting against. Keep in mind that this word "friendship," though it may seem casual to us today, was a serious word describing close intimacy in the context in which James was writing (Moo, *James*, 187). James tells us that friendship with the world causes conflict with others, conflict within yourself, and ultimately conflict with God. James is talking about fights and quarrels in the church in chapter 4, and I can't help but think that the adversary had succeeded in getting these churches to fight with one another to the extent that they lost sight of where the true battle was. As we focus on battling with the world—a world system that encourages us to want more stuff, to prioritize our comforts, and to ignore the poor while we focus on ourselves, the adversary would like nothing more than to divide us so that we fight battles among ourselves and have little energy for the real battle that is going on. We must fervently resist friendship with the world.

Friendship with the world **comes from the sinful desires of the flesh**. In verse 1 James talks about desires that battle within each of us. We want selfish gain, pleasure in this world, and that which is best for us. The problem is that putting people together who all have these sinful, selfish desires creates fights and quarrels. Isn't this the picture of marriage? When you put two selfish sinners together, you certainly aren't going to get perfect peace all the time. These quarrels James talks about get serious when it comes to our relationships, whether it's marriage or friends or in the church. James says, "You murder and covet" (v. 2), which is almost certainly hyperbole; i.e., there probably wasn't first-degree murder taking place within the church. But it does take us back to the Sermon on the Mount where Jesus equated anger between brothers with murder (Matt 5:21-22). Sinful desires are dangerous.

All conflict comes from desires within us, desires that are **motivated by a longing for earthly pleasure**. You're not going to God in prayer, James says to these believers, or if you are, you are going to Him in order to get more in this world for yourself, which misses the point (v. 3). Even the prayers of these people were self-centered. Jesus, on the other hand, taught us to begin prayer like this: "Your name be honored as holy" (Matt 6:9). We are to seek what is best for the sake of God's name. We want His will, not ours, to be done. Friendship with the world says, "My will be done, and my name be great." This is where we realize hostility toward one another is really evidence of hostility toward God. All of this leads to the startling statement in verse 4 concerning friendship with the world.

So far we've seen that friendship with the world comes from the sinful desires of the flesh and that it is motivated by a longing for earthly pleasure. Now in verse 4 we see that friendship with the world **results in spiritual adultery against God**. Throughout this book James has been addressing his hearers as "brothers" (see 1:2,16,19; 2:1,5,14; 3:1,10,12). But then in 4:4 he says, "Adulteresses!" Throughout the Old Testament, God describes His relationship with His people like a marriage, and when His people forsake Him in sin, it is a picture of spiritual unfaithfulness or adultery. In Jeremiah 3:20 God says to His people, "As a woman may betray her lover, so you have betrayed Me, house of Israel" (see also Ezek 16; Hos 1–3). The picture is serious: the more we are conformed to the pattern of this world, living like this world and loving this world, the more we betray our God and cheat on Him. The pain and heartache involved in adultery are wrapped up in this imagery.

In our culture and even in the church, we have sought after the pleasures of this world in sexual immorality, impurity, and debauchery. We have satisfied our flesh with the things of this world with more possessions and nicer cars and bigger houses and better luxuries. We have pursued positions, plaudits, and popularity. We have lived for what is best for us in this world. And in the process, we have run around on our God. We need to repent and come back to Him.

The need to repent helps make sense of James 4:5: "Or do you think it's without reason the Scripture says that the Spirit who lives in us yearns jealously?" There's a lot of debate about how verse 5 should be translated. In light of the context, we should probably understand James to be saying that God jealously longs for the spirit he made to live in us. We're taken back to Exodus 20:5 and 34:14 where God tells His people that He is a jealous God. An illustration may help to explain why this is good news for us. As a husband, I am jealous for the affections of my wife, and anyone or anything that threatens to steal her love from me is met with the strongest of opposition. This is a good thing in marriage; it's the way it's supposed to be. And it's a good thing in our relationship with God that He is jealous for our affections. God is infinitely jealous for His people, and He will oppose with divine force anything or anybody who threatens their good. God is jealous for the affections of your heart as a follower of Christ. This is not an insecure jealousy that is afraid you're going to find someone or something better, for there isn't anyone or anything better. This is a secure jealousy that seeks what is best for you by guarding your heart from adulterous pursuits. He tells us to run from the things of this world and cling to Him in order to find all that we need.

Friendship with God (4:6-10)

Instead of running to friendship and intimacy with this world, we ought to run to friendship with God. This kind of friendship is not birthed in the sinful desires of the flesh, but rather it **comes from the gracious**

desire of God. "[God] gives greater grace" to the humble. As we have had our worldliness exposed in this letter, it is possible for us to look at these truths and commands and feel that it is all too difficult. Yet this is where we see the grace of God. It is not easy to resist the appeal of this world, and there are so many areas where we have bought into this world's friendship. We sometimes wonder whether this struggle will end. However, as Paul tells us in 1 Thessalonians 5:24, "He who calls you is faithful, who also will do it." By God's grace He will produce the fruit of faith in you. Go to Him. Trust in Him. The words of Augustine are appropriate here: "Give me the grace to do as you command, and command me to do what you will" (*Confessions*, 233). God is merciful, gracious, all loving, and He willingly supplies all we need to obey His bold commands. I love what one writer said:

> What comfort there is in this verse! It tells us that God is
> tirelessly on our side. He never falters in respect of our needs,
> he always has *more grace* at hand for us. He is never less than
> sufficient, he always has more and yet more to give. Whatever
> we may forfeit when we put self first, we cannot forfeit our
> salvation, for there is always *more grace*. No matter what we do
> to him, he is never beaten. . . . His resources are never at an
> end, his patience is never exhausted, his initiative never stops,
> his generosity knows no limit: *he gives more grace*. (Motyer,
> *James*, 150; emphasis in original)

Praise God: He gives more grace.

Friendship with God not only comes from the gracious desire of God, but also it **is motivated by a longing for eternal satisfaction**. Friendship with God realizes that if we seek friendship with the world now, we will experience the opposition of God in eternity. Therefore, friendship with God **results in submission to the authority of God**. "Submit to God," James says in verse 7. James lists nine imperative verbs—commands—that tell us what submission looks like. If we want to grow in intimacy with God, these are the things we ought to do:

Resist the Devil forcefully. This is evident in 4:7b. James wants us to stop resisting God and start resisting the Devil. It is baffling that, from the lives of Adam and Eve in Genesis 3 to the lives of every one of us in the present, each of us believes the lies of the Devil. This is the essence of sin—trusting the Devil while distrusting God. Sin is believing the lies of the prince of this world that say we need some thing or person or status, all the while disbelieving God who says, "You need Me." Resist the Devil, and he will flee. Whatever power or influence the Devil may have, your life in Christ is far greater. When you are tempted to go to that site on the Internet, resist him. When you are tempted to speak selfishly to your wife or husband or friend, resist him. When you are tempted to anger, discouragement, doubt, pride, or worry, resist him. Resist him, and he will flee.

Seek God repentantly. In verse 8 James tells us to draw near to God, which implies that we have turned away from Him. This is a call to repent of sin and return to our gracious Lord.

Pursue purity holistically. Purity is both internal and external. James says, "Cleanse your hands, sinners, and purify your hearts" (v. 8). James wants us to purify our hearts, our minds, our desires, our motives, and the core of our being. By God's grace we are to be clean inside and out.

Treat sin seriously. Verse 9 can almost sound depressing: "Be miserable and mourn and weep. Your laughter must change to mourning and your joy to sorrow." Those who live in friendship with this world do not see sin as a big deal. But James tells us not to be trivial with sin. Rather, we should grieve over our sin, mourning and wailing in tears over it. We need to see sin this way. Cornelius Plantinga has talked about how we have lost this view of sin:

> The awareness of sin used to be our shadow. Christians hated sin, feared it, fled from it, grieved over it. Some of our grandparents agonized over their sins. A man who lost his temper might wonder whether he could still go to Holy Communion. A woman who for years envied her more attractive and intelligent sister might wonder if this sin threatened her very salvation.
> But the shadow has dimmed. Nowadays, the accusation *you have sinned* is often said with a grin, and with a tone that signals an inside joke. At one time, this accusation still had the power to jolt people. (Plantinga, *Not the Way*, ix)

D. Martyn Lloyd-Jones has noted how the awareness of sin grew in times of revival:

> Go and read the history of revivals again. Watch the individuals at the beginning. This is invariably the first thing that happens to them. They begin to see what a terrible, appalling thing sin is in the sight of God. They temporarily

even forget the state of the Church, and forget their own anguish. It is the thought of sin in the sight of God. How terrible it must be. Never has there been a revival but that some of the people, especially at the beginning, have had such visions of the holiness of God, and the sinfulness of sin, that they have scarcely known what to do with themselves. (Lloyd-Jones, *Revival*, 157)

When was the last time you grieved over your sin before God? You may think that sounds self-defeating. What about feeling good about yourself and self-esteem? True beauty comes in verse 10, when James says, "Humble yourselves before the Lord, and He will exalt you." When we humble ourselves before God, we don't have to lift ourselves up; He does the lifting for us.

Trust God completely. God will give you grace in your humility, and He will be the one to raise you up. You need not do that on your own.

Two Pictures of Speech
JAMES 4:11-12

When you have been humbled before God, it inevitably affects the way you speak to others. This is where James puts a bookend on the discussion he started at the beginning of chapter 3 regarding the tongue. **Worldly speech** does two things. First, it **discourages one another**. To "criticize" is to speak against, to attack, or to slander another person. Or it can refer to speaking critically to someone else about another person. Gossip and slander will kill community. It is self-centered rather than God centered. Proverbs 6:16-18 says, "The LORD hates six things; in fact, seven are detestable to Him: arrogant eyes, a lying tongue, hands that shed innocent blood, a heart that plots wicked schemes, feet eager to run to evil, a lying witness who gives false testimony, and *one who stirs up trouble among brothers*" (emphasis added).

The second thing worldly speech does is that it **dishonors God**. When you slander, you put yourself above the law of God, as if it is not necessary for you to love your neighbor in the way you speak. In the process you offend the Giver of that law, who is God Himself. Obviously there are places where God says in His Word that it is right and good to confront one another in sin, which can be difficult, but this is done not out of selfish ambition or to hurt your brother, but to help him and to honor God. Criticizing does neither.

Worldly speech discourages one another and dishonors God. **Godly speech**, on the other hand, **encourages one another** and **exalts God.** This is the kind of speech that ought to characterize believers—speech that demonstrates a love of God and neighbor. Out of the overflow of our hearts we want our words to glorify God and to point others to His truth. This is true wisdom. This is what flows from the one who is a friend of God and not a friend of the world.

One Prayer in Faith

O God, for the glory of Christ
amid urgent spiritual and physical need in the world,
we submit our minds, our hearts, our voices, and our lives
to You.

Reflect and Discuss

1. Who in your life has exemplified and imparted godly wisdom? What characteristics mark his or her life?
2. How does the world's definition of wisdom differ from Scripture's definition?
3. According to James 3:13, why can't someone whose life is marked by immorality be considered wise?
4. What's the difference between knowing facts and possessing godly wisdom?
5. Explain what it means to be a friend of the world.
6. What is God's role in keeping us from pursuing sin? What is our role?
7. Practically speaking, what does it mean to submit to God and resist the Devil?
8. How would you define repentance for someone who has no Bible knowledge?
9. How is it in James 4:11 that speaking evil against a brother is speaking evil against the law?
10. How is intentionally engaging unbelievers different from pursuing friendship with the world?

Faith Lasts

JAMES 4:13–5:20

Main Idea: Faith that perseveres to the end is humble before the sovereignty of God, obedient to the will of God, confident in the justice of God, patient in suffering, trustworthy in speech, prayerful in sorrow, and loving toward sinners.

I. **Faith That Perseveres**
   A. Humble before the sovereignty of God (4:13-16)
   B. Obedient to the will of God (4:17)
   C. Confident in the justice of God (5:1-7)
      1. He is coming to judge the sinful.
      2. He is coming to deliver the faithful.
   D. Patient in suffering (5:7-11)
   E. Trustworthy in speech (5:12)
   F. Prayerful in sorrow (5:13-18)
   G. Loving toward sinners (5:19-20)
II. **Faith That Works**
   A. Only possible by the gracious gospel of Christ
   B. Played out in the context of the body of Christ
   C. Ultimately aimed toward great glory to Christ

When preaching through this epistle, a brother in Christ told me that he was so thankful for James and all that it was doing in his life and in the life of our church. Then he said, "What I'm most thankful for is that James only has five chapters." This brother had discovered something to which many Christians can testify: James turns our lives in this world upside down. But it does this for the good of God's people and for the good of God's glory among the lost and the poor.

Different books of the Bible cause different effects in our lives and in the life of the church. Books like Ruth are going to comfort us, while books like James are going to challenge us. As long as we let the Word do the speaking and the leading, we can know that God is going to do what is best for us as His people, what is best for those around us who are without Him, and ultimately what is best for His glory in all the world.

His Word is good, and we can trust it—every bit of it—even when it's difficult. If I had to sum up this last part of the book of James, I would say
this is a picture of faith that perseveres.

Faith That Perseveres

In James 4:13–5:20 we see seven characteristics of persevering faith.

Humble Before the Sovereignty of God (4:13-16)

Business travel in the first century was actually fairly common, and verse
13 pictures a businessman confidently planning to make a profit in the
future. James calls talking about your business affairs as if they are cer-
tainties "boasting" or bragging, that is, doing things in your own strength
without admitting dependence on God. James is warning us that **we can
become so consumed with the material realm**, thinking about our plans,
plots, and strategies to work and make money, **that we become blind
to spiritual realities**. The problem is not the planning in and of itself
but planning in such a way that God has no place in the plans. James
is referring to a situation in which these people were arranging to do
something in the coming year in order to make money, when the reality
is that they didn't even know if they're going to see tomorrow! These
people were acting as if all their plans were certain, but they were living
in arrogance, not acknowledging that their breath could be taken away
in an instant. **God is sovereign over life and death**. Your life is a mist, a
smoke (v. 14). Your life is like a vapor, here one second and gone the
next, and you will live until tomorrow only if the Lord wills. What a humbling reminder this is: not one of us is guaranteed that we will be alive
tonight to lay our head on our pillow.

God is sovereign over life and death **and over our activities and our
accomplishments**. "If the Lord wills, we will live and do this or that" (v.
15). Everything we do, everything we accomplish, and everything we
attain is ultimately under the sovereign will of God. Now the intent here
is not to create a passive fatalism in our minds that says, "Well, God has
determined everything, so I'm just going to sit back and do nothing
and see what He decides to do." No, remember that James gives plenty
of commands to obey and actions to take. James is talking about activity throughout this book, but he's talking about activity that is humbly
dependent on the sovereign God of the universe. Every accomplish-
ment and every activity, literally every breath, is acknowledging, "I am

alive, and I am working only by the sovereign grace of God." James isn't saying that before we do anything, we always need to say out loud, "If the Lord wills" (though saying it often wouldn't hurt us). The point is to have a mind-set that says, "I need the grace of God, and I am dependent on the will of God in every facet of my life."

James describes a radically different way to live in this world, particularly in the busyness and the business of our lives. This world tells us to live like we're going to be here forever, urging us to make our plans, acquire our possessions, and work to build our portfolio. But James tells us to submit to God. Don't live like you're going to be here forever. Instead, live and plan and work like your life is short and like you don't want to waste it on worldly things. Live like you want to spend your life humbly before the sovereignty of God and ultimately for the glory of God. As the people of God, we ought to make our lives—the mist that comprises who you are for the short while you are here—count under His sovereignty for His glory. Be finished and done with self-sufficiency in this life, and live your lives radically dependent on the sovereignty of God.

Obedient to the Will of God (4:17)

James says, "So it is a sin for the person who knows to do what is good and doesn't do it." Humble submission to God's will means humble obedience to God's will. This is where James gives us a needed perspective on sin.

We normally think of sin in terms of **sins of commission: doing what God has said not to do.** God says, "Do not lie," and so you do not lie. God says, "Do not covet," and so you do not covet. This is how we often think of sin—as not doing bad things. But James reminds us that just as serious as lying or coveting or doing anything else that God has said not to do are **sins of omission: disregarding what God has said to do.** This involves hearing the command of God to do something—such as the command to admit dependence on God when you make your business plans—and then choosing not to do it.

Reviewing all we have studied up to this point, we see how James told us not to show favoritism. Consequently, it would be a sin of *commission* for us to show favoritism. But he's also told us to care for the needy. Therefore, it would be sin of *omission* for us not to care for the needy. In fact, this is how Jesus approached lack of care for the needy. At the end of Matthew 25, people are cast into hell, not because of what they

did but because of what they didn't do. They didn't feed the hungry
or clothe the naked. They failed to do what God has commanded His
people to do all along—to care for those in need (Matt 25:31-46; Moo,
James, 208).

To make the seriousness of sins of omission more clear, imagine
someone who claims to be a Christian but lives in sexual immorality.
Even when confronted with the Word over and over again—the Word
that says not to commit sexual immorality (Rom 13:13) and to flee sexual immorality (1 Cor 6:18)—he deliberately does what God has said
not to do. This is eternally serious sin, especially when God says the
sexually immoral will not inherit the kingdom of God (1 Cor 6:9; Gal
5:19-21; Eph 5:5). But what about the person who sees repeatedly in
God's Word that we should care for the poor, particularly our brothers
and sisters in Christ who are poor, and does nothing? If we continually
ignore and disregard this command, then according to James, this too is
sin. And the consequences are just as severe. As we've seen, in Matthew
25 Jesus actually tells people who have ignored the poor to depart into
the eternal fire prepared for the Devil and his angels! This should cause
us to realize that it is eternally serious to ignore the poor. Faith that lasts
is obedient to the will of God.

Confident in the Justice of God (5:1-7)

James's emphasis on the poor leads to the harshest language in the
entire book. The tone at the end of chapter 4 has carried over into the
rebuke of the rich in these verses. James emphasizes the fact that the
judgment of God is coming soon. Verse 1 mentions "miseries that are
coming," verse 3 refers to the "last days," and verse 5 alludes to a "day
of slaughter." This emphasis on God's end-time judgment continues in
verses 7-9: James says to "be patient until the Lord's coming" (v. 7); in
verse 8 he says that "the Lord's coming is near"; then in verse 9 we learn
that the "judge stands at the door!" Jesus is coming back, and He's going
to do at least two things.

He is coming to judge the sinful. These first six verses of James 5 are
most likely addressed to unbelievers. These people are not called brothers. They are only told to weep and wail, and the language is similar
to what the prophets would pronounce on pagan nations (Moo, *James*,
210). You might wonder why, in a book addressed to Christians, James
would spend time using such harsh language toward unbelievers. The
answer is that he is reminding the Christians that the justice of God

is coming. This reality should enable them to be patient. With that said, that doesn't mean these verses don't have any other application to Christians. James has already rebuked Christian brothers and sisters who were favoring the rich above the poor, so 5:1-6 serves as both a direct rebuke to rich nonbelievers who were oppressing the poor and a subtle, indirect warning to rich believers (Christians) who were ignoring the poor. Notice that James is not necessarily condemning wealth here; instead, he focuses on the sinful use of wealth. At the same time, for those of us who are part of a culture that is extremely wealthy compared to the rest of the world, we need to examine whether or not we are engaged in a sinful use of the resources God has given us.

James brings four accusations against the unbelieving rich. First, they were going to be judged **for hoarding wealth** (5:2-3). The rich were storing away their wealth in barns (to use an image from Jesus' teachings), and James says all that money and all those possessions—all the stuff you buy that you do not need—is rotting. You think your investments are wise, James says, but they are wasting away. Moths are eating your clothes, and your gold is corroding. Some have pointed out that this is not possible because gold doesn't corrode like iron does. But that's the point: James is saying that even that which you think is the surest use of money in this world is wasting away. You have hoarded and built bigger barns for all of your excess, but a day is coming when it is all going to burn up in the fire, and you will burn up with it.

These believers were hoarding up wealth as they prepared to meet the eternal Judge, and their hoarded resources would testify against them. **Their treasures on earth would bring about their torment in eternity.** Recall Jesus' parable in Luke 12:13-21:

> *Someone from the crowd said to Him, "Teacher, tell my brother to divide the inheritance with me."*
>
> *"Friend," He said to him, "who appointed Me a judge or arbitrator over you?" He then told them, "Watch out and be on guard against all greed because one's life is not in the abundance of his possessions."*
>
> *Then He told them a parable: "A rich man's land was very productive. He thought to himself, 'What should I do, since I don't have anywhere to store my crops? I will do this,' he said. 'I'll tear down my barns and build bigger ones and store all my grain and my goods there. Then I'll say to myself, "You have many goods stored up for many years. Take it easy; eat, drink, and enjoy yourself."'*

> *"But God said to him, 'You fool! This very night your life is demanded of you. And the things you have prepared—whose will they be?'*
>
> *"That's how it is with the one who stores up treasure for himself and is not rich toward God."*

Be wary of storing up "treasures on earth, where moth and rust destroy and where thieves break in and steal. But collect for yourselves treasures in heaven, where neither moth nor rust destroys, and where thieves don't break in and steal" (Matt 6:19-20).

James's hearers would also be judged **for cheating workers**. In that day there was a concentration of land in the hands of small numbers of wealthy landowners. If the landowners were selfish or delayed in paying their workers, it was not uncommon for the workers to struggle severely, being unable to get daily food or drink. **The possessions of the rich were accumulating while other people were dying.**

Next these individuals would be judged **for living in self-indulgence.** Do you see the imagery in verse 5? These rich people were like cattle gorging on food on the day of their slaughter. May God help us in our materialistic culture to see the warning in this imagery. May we not be like cows enjoying all our stuff, unaware that we're about to be destroyed. We're reminded of the description of Sodom and Gomorrah in Ezekiel 16:49, where the people had "pride, plenty of food, and comfortable security, but didn't support the poor and needy" (Moo, *James,* 217). **They were overfed and unconcerned.** Is there any clearer imagery for a culture where wealth is so concentrated while literally thousands around the world die every day because they do not have food or water?

The ultimate picture here is that the rich would be judged **for condemning men.** Strikingly, one commentator explained, "In the Jewish world, to deprive a person of their support was the same as murdering them" (Blomberg and Kamell, *James,* 225). This is what the unbelieving rich were doing, and ultimately, **their oppression of others would lead to their own damnation.** This is aimed at unbelievers, but as God's people we need to pause for a moment to feel the weight of this. Of all people, God is certainly serious about His people not hoarding wealth, not cheating workers, not living in luxury and self-indulgence, and not holding back from the poor and in effect letting them die.

He is coming to deliver the faithful. Now for a moment put yourself in the shoes of struggling, impoverished, persecuted Christians who might be reading this letter. You hear the Word of God toward the unbelieving rich, and you know that He is coming to judge the sinful, but even more than that, you realize He is coming to deliver the faithful. In verse 4 James refers to the "Lord of Hosts," or the Master of Armies, and he's telling his hearers that their cries and their pain are heard on high. The Lord of Hosts will vindicate you in due time. This is why James says in verse 7 to "be patient until the Lord's coming." He is coming to judge the sinful and to deliver the faithful.

Patient in Suffering (5:7-11)

The theme of this part of the letter is clear: patience is mentioned twice in verse 7 and once each in verses 8 and 10 while the words "endured" and "endurance" are used in verse 11. James gives us three pictures of patience to encourage us.

First, he says to be patient **like a farmer: waiting for the harvest**. In an agricultural society you live dependent on God's provision in the weather. Too much rain can causes the crop to rot, too little rain causes drought, and frost kills the crop. Talk about needing patience! The illustration of a farmer reminds us that faith involves **trusting God with what you cannot control**. A farmer cannot determine when it will rain and when it will not. So, James says, when it comes to the Lord's coming and the injustice that surrounds you, like a farmer trust God with what you cannot control while **honoring God with what you can control**. James mentions in verse 9 that they were grumbling against one another. While we wait patiently and endure trials, we will be tempted to sin. We will be tempted to complain and speak evil against one another, but we must resist this. Remember, the Judge is coming (v. 9), and we want to be found faithful with what we can control. Like a farmer trust that the harvest God brings in His time will be worth the wait.

Second, we are to be patient **like a prophet: speaking the truth**. Much like the farmer, the prophet reminds us that patience does not necessarily mean inactivity. A farmer doesn't just sit back waiting for the rain: he works. Likewise, a prophet in the middle of persecution stood boldly and spoke out against injustice. In the middle of hardship, we are to speak about the goodness, the greatness, the judgment, and the mercy of God. Times of suffering are often the most golden opportunity to speak a word for the glory of God.

Third, we need patience **like Job: hoping in God's purpose**. James says, "You have heard of Job's endurance and have seen the outcome from the Lord" (Jas 5:11). What an understatement! Remember that it took 42 chapters for the purpose of suffering in Job's life to be revealed, and only at the end did he confess, "I had heard rumors about You, but now my eyes have seen You. Therefore I take back my words and repent in dust and ashes" (Job 42:5-6). This is a good reminder for us: Whatever you are walking through is not the end of the story. The end will reveal that the Lord is indeed "very compassionate and merciful" (Jas 5:11). You can't see it, but be patient, hoping in God's purpose.

Trustworthy in Speech (5:12)

In verse 12 James takes what seems like a hard left and starts talking about oaths. He says, "Your 'yes' must be 'yes,' and your 'no' must be 'no,' so that you won't fall under judgment." This is important, particularly in light of all that we have seen about our tongues in James. He is saying faith that perseveres is trustworthy in speech. The words from our mouths should be so consistent and dependable that they guarantee reliability.

Prayerful in Sorrow (5:13-18)

James goes back to the struggles he left off with in verses 7-11, and he says faith that perseveres is prayerful in sorrow. Much as we saw with the theme of patience in the preceding verses, prayer is all over this section, mentioned in every verse. James again reminds us that patience does not involve just sitting back doing nothing. This is not a passive waiting but an active waiting. He says to **pray when you are hurting**, and the context here includes all different kinds of trouble—spiritual, physical, emotional, financial, etc. The patience in suffering that James has talked about only comes from God, and prayer is the way to obtain it.

Not only do you pray when you are hurting, but you **pray when you are happy**. Our prayers ought also to be filled with God's praise as we consider His goodness and grace.

In verse 14 James says to **pray with the elders**: "Is anyone among you sick? He should call for the elders of the church, and they should pray over him after anointing him with olive oil in the name of the Lord." The indication is that someone is weak and bedridden in such a way that they could not get out easily to gather together with the church. Therefore, the elders, or pastors, who shepherd the body would come, at the invitation of a brother or sister, to pray over him.

The emphasis here is clearly on praying, but James also mentions the elders anointing the sick brother or sister with oil. Historically, there has been a lot of discussion about the significance of this anointing with oil.[15] Some have wondered, "**Is the oil medicinal?**" Oil had common medicinal uses in that day, so this verse could be telling us to pray over sick people and give them medicine. But there's a problem with this view: while oil may have had common medicinal purposes in that day, this word was never used in the Greek version of the Old Testament to refer to medicine.[16] Certainly other medicinal salves would have been used with other specific illnesses, but why would the elders be the ones to administer medical care? Surely someone else could or would have given medicine to a person who was sick.

Others have wondered, "**Is the oil sacramental?**" The anointing with oil developed into a sacrament practiced by the Catholic Church that would remove remnants of sin and strengthen the soul in preparation for death. This is something that would be administered by a priest, often just before someone dies. This clearly doesn't have a basis in this text because the focus is on prayer for healing.

My humble opinion is that **the oil is symbolic**. It is common in Scripture to see anointing that symbolizes setting apart someone or something for a particular purpose. In most of the Old Testament uses of the word *anoint*, the word refers to the consecration of something. A variety of different interpretations are clearly possible here, but ultimately the power for healing is not found in any oil but in the God who answers prayer. While the elders pray over someone, the oil symbolizes setting them apart for special attention and care from God.

The important thing to note is that this is not an extremely significant sticking point. This is the only place in the New Testament letters where anointing a sick person with oil is even mentioned, and many healings occurred without anointing. The emphasis is on praying and not just to pray with the elders but, according to James 5:16, to **pray with the church**. Yes, the elders play a special role in the case of someone who is bedridden and cannot gather together with the church, but the emphasis in verse 16 is on praying with one another and for one another. No special power is reserved for the elders: the power is in God, and it is available to the praying church. Care and prayer for one another are not just intended to happen within the context of leadership in the

---

[15] For the discussion of verse 14 below and the options mentioned, see Moo, *The Letter of James*, 238–42.

[16] The Greek version of the Old Testament is referred to as the Septuagint, or LXX.

church but in the context of the church as a whole. When we are sick, we call on one another to pray, not just this or that leader.

In verse 16 James also says to "**confess your sins to one another.**" Interestingly, this is the only verse in the New Testament that commands believers to confess their sins to one another (Moo, *James*, 246), and this command is given in the context of praying for the healing of one another. When we think about the relationship between prayer and confession of sin in James, clearly the implication is that if a person has sinned against a brother, he should confess the sin to him. We know from Scripture that **sin directly causes some sickness.** For example, taking the Lord's Supper in an unworthy manner caused some in Corinth to become weak and sick, and others had even died (1 Cor 11:30). So it's important to pray and examine whether any sin has caused sickness.

But I would warn against taking this too far. Yes, sin can directly cause some sickness but not necessarily all sickness. Just because someone has a particular illness does not automatically mean that person has sinned in some way. Jesus, James, and the rest of the New Testament counter this idea.[17] James says in verse 15, "If he has committed sins, he will be forgiven." But at the same time, the whole of Scripture does teach that **sin indirectly causes all sickness.** Sickness and death are both ultimately the result of the fall and its effect on the world. Moreover, when we are sick, even if sin did not directly cause our sickness, the temptation to sin when we are physically weak can sometimes be much more potent than when we are physically strong.

Along with confessing sins to one another, a community of faith ought to **intercede on behalf of one another.** All followers of Christ need to be involved with brothers and sisters with whom they can confess sins and struggles and pray for one another. However, in light of verse 15a, does this mean that if you pray with enough faith someone will be healed? And if they are not healed, does that mean that you did not pray with enough faith? Obviously, experience says differently. I have been in situations with the elders at my church where we have prayed for a brother or sister and they were healed. In other situations the same elders have said the same kinds of prayers for a brother or sister, and they were not healed. Practically, I would not in any way say to

---

[17] For example, see Jesus' reply to His disciples about the man born blind in John 9:1-3.

any of the families who have lost loved ones that they were not praying with enough faith. There are clearly practical and experiential reasons for not linking sickness too closely with our prayers and our faith. But are there biblical reasons as well? What does Scripture say about this? The answer is found in the example James gives next.

James's example of Elijah in 5:17 points out that our faith must always be in accordance with God's promises. Everything Elijah did in 1 Kings 17 and 18 was in accordance with God's Word. God said it would not rain, and it didn't, and then God said rain was coming, and it did. The beauty is that God used Elijah's prayers as the means through which His Word was accomplished. Elijah didn't demand that God do something He was reluctant to do; rather, Elijah prayed in accordance with God's Word, trusting that God would keep His promises.

So when it comes to praying for the sick—for a brother or sister who has cancer or some other illness—do we have a word from God about whether they will live? No. In fact, God told Paul on one occasion that He would not heal him (2 Cor 12:7-10). Paul says, "I pleaded with the Lord three times to take it away from me. But He said to me, 'My grace is sufficient for you, for power is perfected in weakness'" (2 Cor 12:8). It was clearly not God's will to take away this thorn.

But, someone might wonder, doesn't Jesus say that if we ask Him for anything, He will do it? This question refers to John 14:14, where Jesus said, "If you ask Me anything in My name, I will do it." This phrase "in My name" uncovers the answer, for it helps us learn **the secret to power and effectiveness in prayer**. To ask for something in the name of Christ is to ask for something according to His Word and for His glory. So when you pray, you need to start by **making your wants God's wants**. You express your desire to see the Word of Christ in action and the name of Christ exalted. And when that is the driving force behind your prayers, then you can (and should!) **ask for whatever you want**, trusting that He desires to put His Word into action in order to bring praise to the Father. Now in some situations you or I may not know precisely what God wants (i.e., whether He will heal a person). But we are free to express our desires to Him according to His Word, all the while asking Him to change our desires to accord with His will. And as we pray, we trust Him to bring about that which is best for us and most glorifying for Him.

Loving Toward Sinners (5:19-20)

This is the seventh and final characteristic of faith that lasts. As we come to the end of this book—this letter filled with all kinds of commands, warnings, and practical instructions—James says to the church, in light of all these things, to look out for one another. Brothers and sisters will wander from these commands and from the gospel, and the key is for the brothers and sisters to be there to help them come back. It is not just important that we obey God's commands as individuals. Churches are communities of faith, and God intends us to help spur one another on in obedience to God's commands.

James speaks about **earthly restoration** in verse 19, which is critically important as we work out our faith in community. The work of restoring an erring brother or sister **saves souls**, for James says it will "save his life from death" and **cover sins** (v. 20). Of course, God alone does the actual saving (4:12). Yet, as He saves and sustains us to the end, He uses other believers in the process. But this raises an important question: Are Christians in danger of spiritual and eternal death—of not being saved from their sins?

This is where we realize something extremely significant about **eternal security**. Eternal security is the doctrine, or the truth, that a Christian's salvation is secure for all of eternity. What the whole of the New Testament teaches is that **eternal security is always a certainty**. When you trust in Christ as Savior and Lord to cover over your sins and make you right before God, you are adopted into His family, and you are His child forever. That is a certainty to which Scripture consistently bears witness. But the question is, How does God keep us in His family? That is, how does God guard us from ever wandering away from Him? How does God preserve our salvation to the end? The answer James gives to the church is, "Through you." **Eternal security is accomplished through community**. How does God preserve His people? The answer is, in part, through His people. The church is one of the God-ordained means God uses to keep us faithful. God is sovereign, and He does the preserving, but He does it through the church looking out for, caring for, and loving one another to keep one another from sin. This is yet another reason we ought to be involved in the lives of others in the church. God has ordained brothers and sisters who will share life with you to keep you close to Him, to keep you obedient to His commands, and to preserve you until the Lord comes back.

Faith That Works

We come now to a brief summary of the book of James, and we'll focus on three important themes that have come up in these five chapters.

First, faith that works is **only possible by the gracious gospel of Christ**. As I was working on this section of James, one of my sons climbed up in my lap and asked if I was working on my sermon. I told him I was, and I asked him what he thought I should preach on.

He said, "Jesus."

So I asked, "What should I tell them about Jesus?"

He said, "Tell them that Jesus said to be kind to others."

I asked, "How can they be kind?"

He responded, "They can share with their friends."

"What can they share?" I wondered out loud.

He said, "They can share their toys and their Mack trucks and their cars and their books and their puzzles and their vegetables."

"Why should they share, buddy?" I finally asked him.

His response? "Because Jesus died on a cross to save them from their sins."

This is it. This is gospel obedience. We obey the commands of Christ throughout the book of James through the power of the One who died on the cross for our sins.

This faith that works is only possible by the gracious gospel of Christ, and second, it is **played out in the context of the body of Christ**. James repeatedly addresses his hearers as "brothers,"[18] which indicates that he is not simply addressing individuals. He is referring to the family of faith gathered together. Faith is lived out together, not in isolation. Whether it is walking through trials, seeking after wisdom, using our tongues, or caring for the poor, it all happens in the context of the body of Christ.

Finally, faith that works is **ultimately aimed toward great glory to Christ**. May God deliver us from a faith that doesn't work. Not only has Christ died to give us so much more, but the world around us is looking for so much more. What kind of difference does Christ make in your life? Let's show the world a radically different way to live—as salt and light—so that they might see our lives and give great glory to the One who has saved us.

---

[18] James refers to his hearers as "brothers" 15 times.

Reflect and Discuss

1. How can planning for the future be wise? How can it become sinful? What's the difference?
2. How does greed blind us to spiritual realities? Where have you seen this show up in your own life?
3. Why are sins of omission so much easier to downplay than sins of commission? What are some specific struggles in your life in terms of scriptural commands you tend to ignore?
4. What are some specific ways in which materialism and covetousness show up in your own life?
5. According to James 5:1-11, why is it so detrimental to our faith to abandon a belief in Christ's return and final judgment? How should this truth affect our outlook on life while we wait?
6. Is the patience James calls for different from inactivity? Explain.
7. Why is faith in God's character so crucial in our suffering? How is Job a model in this regard?
8. In what ways are you tempted to compromise your integrity by going back on your word?
9. What role does the body of Christ play in praying for one another?
10. Explain the following statement: Faith that works is only possible by the gracious gospel of Christ.

WORKS CITED

"The AFCARS Report." U.S. Department of Health and HumanServices. Accessed April 3, 2014. http: //www.acf.hhs.go/sites/default/files/cb/afcarsreport20.pdf.

Augustine. *Confessions*. Penguin Classics. Translated by R. S. Pine-Coffin. New York: Penguin, 1961.

BDAG (F. W. Danker, W. Bauer, W. F. Arndt, F. W. Gingrich). *A Greek-English Lexicon of the New Testament and Other Early Christian Literature*, rev. and ed. 3rd ed. Chicago/London: University of Chicago, 2000.

Blomberg, Craig, and Mariam J. Kamell. *James*. Zondervan Exegetical Commentary on the New Testament. Grand Rapids, MI: Zondervan, 2008.

Doriani, Daniel M. *James*. Reformed Expository Commentary. Phillipsburg, NJ: P & R Publishing, 2007.

Empty Tomb. "Giving Research." Accessed March 13, 2014. http://www.emptytomb.org/fig1_07.html.

Johnson, Luke K. *The Letter of James*. Anchor Bible Commentary 37A. New York: Doubleday, 1995.

Keirkegaard, Søren. *Attack Upon "Christendom."* Translated by Walter Lowrie. Princeton, NJ: Princeton University Press, 1968.

Keller, Timothy J. *Ministries of Mercy: The Call of the Jericho Road*. 2nd edition. Phillipsburg: P&R Publishing, 1997.

Laws, Sophie. *The Epistle of James*. Black's New Testament Commentary. Grand Rapids, MI: Baker Academic, 1993.

Lloyd-Jones, Martyn. *Revival*. Wheaton, IL: Crossway, 1987.

Luther, Martin. *Luther's Works*. Edited by Jarislov Pelikan, et al. Philadelphia: Fortress, 1958–1995.

Moo, Douglas J. *The Letter of James*. The Pillar New Testament Commentary. Grand Rapids, MI: Eerdmans, 2000.

Motyer, J. A. *The Message of James*. The Bible Speaks Today. Downers Grove, IL: InterVarsity, 1985.

Muggeridge, Malcolm. *A Twentieth Century Testimony*. Nashville, TN: Thomas Nelson, 1978.

Plantinga, Cornelius. *Not the Way It's Supposed to Be: A Breviary of Sin*. Grand Rapids, MI: Eerdmans, 1995.

Platt, David. *Radical: Taking Back Your Faith from the American Dream.* Colorado Springs, CO: Multnomah, 2010.

———. *Radical Together: Unleashing the People of God for the Purpose of God.* Colorado Springs, CO: Multnomah, 2011.

Ronsvalle, John, and Sylvia Ronsvalle. *The State of Church Giving Through 2003.* 15th ed. Champaign, IL: Empty Tomb, 2005.

Spurgeon, Charles Haddon. "Before Sermon, at Sermon, and after Sermon." Sermon 1847 in volume 31 of *The Metropolitan Tabernacle Pulpit.* Accessed Feb. 6, 2013. http://www.ccel.org/ccel/spurgeon/sermons31.xxxii.html.

———. "The Final Separation: A Sermon on Matthew 25:32." Sermon 1234 in volume 21 of *The Metropolitan Tabernacle Pulpit.* Accessed March 13, 2014. http://www.ccel.org/ccel/spurgeon/sermons21.xxv.html.

Stein, Robert H. "Saved by Faith [Alone] in Paul Versus 'Not Saved by Faith Alone' in James." *Southern Baptist Journal of Theology* 4 (2000): 4–14.

Yun, Brother, Peter Xu Yongze, and Enoch Wang with Paul Hattaway. *Back to Jerusalem: Three Chinese House Church Leaders Share Their Vision to Complete the Great Commission.* Downers Grove, IL: InterVarsity, 2003.

SCRIPTURE INDEX